Understanding, Assessing, and Intervening on

READING PROBLEMS

A Guide for School Psychologists and Other Educational Consultants

LAURICE M. JOSEPH, PhD

Ohio State University

From the NASP Publications Board Operations Manual

The content of this document reflects the ideas and positions of the authors. The responsibility lies solely with the authors and does not necessarily reflect the position or ideas of the National Association of School Psychologists.

Published by the National Association of School Psychologists

Copies may be ordered from:
NASP Publications
4340 East West Highway, Suite 402
Bethesda, MD 20814
(301) 657-0270
(301) 657-0275, fax
e-mail: *publications@naspweb.org*
www.nasponline.org

ISBN-13: 978-0-932955-76-0 and ISBN-10: 0-932955-76-2

Printed in the United States of America

First Printing, Fall 2006

10 9 8 7 6 5 4 3 2 1

Dedication

I dedicate this book to my parents, Ellis and Guitta, siblings, Ellis Jr. and Paula, Aunts Vera and Rose, and Uncles Nassif and George, who encouraged me and supported my passion to read and learn throughout my personal and professional journey.

I also dedicate this book to my loving grandparents, Ab and Marie Joseph and Nassif and Laurice Cannon for not only making the journey to the United States of America and making it their home but for valuing its greatest ideals, which made it possible for their family to fulfill all their personal and professional dreams. Although they are no longer with me in this life, I know they share this accomplishment with me in a better life!

Table of Contents

Acknowledgments

First and foremost, I wish to express my gratitude and appreciation to the National Association of School Psychologists Publications Board for supporting my efforts in completing this book. Special thanks are given to Nancy Metzler Peterson, Denise Ferrenz, and Linda Morgan. I would also like to express sincere thanks to Joe Gerard, who provided extremely helpful feedback, kept me on task, and championed my work throughout this endeavor. I also wish to thank Dr. Matt Burns for his insightful critical review of and feedback on many chapters.

Work of this magnitude and my own developmental process as a writer, scholar, and academician did not come about alone. I have been fortunate to have the encouragement and the opportunities provided by many of my colleagues over the years, which made arriving at a stage to create this work possible. There are many who have influenced me, but I would like to especially thank those who provided me with opportunities to contribute in scholarly and practical ways to the professions of school psychology and reading. I first would like to thank Dr. Andrea Canter, who invited a once-beginning academician to write and become a reviewer for the *Communiqué* and has since provided me with several opportunities to contribute to my profession. This has certainly contributed to my growth. Next, I wish to express gratitude to Drs. Ed Daly and Christopher Skinner. Although I have not been one of their students, their work in school psychology, with their particular focus on academic interventions and experimental analysis, has inspired me and made me realize that there is so much yet to discover and learn about reading.

There is that rare, scientifically minded, caring, and kind professional who enters your academic life and "looks after" your well-being and makes it possible for you to experience success, and for me that person is Dr. William Mike Sherman, former department chair and current vice provost of academic affairs at Ohio State University. My potential as an academician was realized in more ways than I had ever imagined as he created the right conditions and nurtured me from an assistant to an associate professor so that I might engage in an endeavor of this kind. I also wish to sincerely thank the current chair of my department, Dr. Donna Pastore, who has supported my work and who is an outstanding scholarly mentor, shaping me to become an academic leader in my profession.

I thank many wonderful faculty colleagues at OSU but give extra thanks to my lifelong mentors, Drs. John Cooper, Tim Heron, and Bill Heward, who have made my academic life since the time I was a student until now a most rewarding, positive, and intellectually stimulating experience. I will carry on their teachings through demonstration, modeling, feedback, reinforcement, and opportunities to engage in scholarship throughout my entire career. My hat is also tipped to my lifelong mentors and friends, Jill and Bob Simmons, special education directors, who model best reading practices for children in the everyday world of professional practice.

As a doctoral student, I was fortunate to work in the reading clinic at Ohio State University with an incredible reading expert and scholar, Dr. Sandra McCormick. There I witnessed the implementation and effects of evidence-based reading interventions with individual students.

In saving the best for last, I confess I would not be driven to do the work that I do on a day-to-day basis if it were not for the students at Ohio State University, especially those in school psychology and special education. I appreciate each and every one for keeping me reading and learning. I would like to particularly thank Lindsay Nist, Melissa Schmidgall, Jackie Jackson, Timothy Bradenhop, Kimberly Hendry, Megan McCachran, and Kristen McCleod, my advisees, who have worked countless hours, days, and weeks with me on research projects in exploring the effectiveness of reading interventions. There is always that one doctoral student who comes along who shares that deep passion about the field of reading and school psychology, and that student is Rebecca Schisler. I am most grateful to her for taking on the leadership roles of supervising students and assisting with grant-funded research projects and my courses at OSU, which allowed me to devote more time and energy to this wonderful endeavor.

Children, especially those who have struggled and later became proficient readers, have taught me the most about the art and science of learning to read; ultimately, it is for them that I have written this book.

About the Author

Laurice M. Joseph is an Associate Professor of School Psychology at Ohio State University in Columbus, Ohio. She obtained her doctorate in School Psychology with a specialization in Reading at Ohio State University in 1997. During her doctoral studies, she served as a supervisor in the Reading Clinic at OSU under the directorship of Drs. Sandra McCormick and Jerry Zutell. Before obtaining her doctorate, she practiced as a school psychologist for five years in Hardin County Schools, Kenton, Ohio. She earned her master's degree in school psychology and special education at Ohio State University in 1988 and her bachelor's degree in elementary and special education at the University of Dayton in 1985. She has written articles and book chapters and has presented workshops and research papers on reading interventions for school psychologists and related professionals at national and international conferences. She was selected as a P-12 outreach and engagement scholar and awarded funding in 2005 at Ohio State University for her work on examining the effectiveness of reading interventions for children who were in need of intensive reading services. Her most recent research involves determining effective as well as efficient reading interventions on word reading skill acquisition, fluency, and comprehension for learners with special needs.

Preface

When I began my journey in the professional practice of school psychology, I soon came to realize how little I knew about a problem, an epidemic really, that many of our nation's children faced. The problem so many of the children who were referred to me faced was that of becoming literate. Literacy determines one's ability to function successfully in school and in society. During this early time, I knew very little about how reading developed or evidence-based reading interventions. As a consultant on intervention assistant teams, I often provided suggestions that seemed to be logical and feasible without knowing whether or not my suggestions were targeting children's needs. I decided that I needed to become more knowledgeable about teaching children how to read and to pursue doctoral studies in school psychology with a specialization in reading.

Since I obtained my doctorate, I have worked as a faculty member doing research in the area of reading; I have worked with children and professionals in school districts, especially in the area of reading interventions; and I have come to learn a great deal about how reading develops, how to assess children's literacy needs, and how to teach children to progress as readers. One of my greatest passions has been to share what I know with school psychologists and other professionals working in consultant roles so that they will be in a position to be more resourceful than I had been during my early practice. Therefore, this book is designed for the practitioner, with the intention to provide school psychologists and other educational consultants with an understanding of how reading develops, how to assess reading development and link that information to intervention, and how to teach reading using evidence-based approaches.

The book is divided into two sections. The first section describes ecological factors that contribute to the development of reading skills and discusses diverse types of learners. In this section, a variety of assessment tools are discussed, along with how those tools can be used in targeting interventions to address specific literacy needs of children. Section two describes effective instructional components and approaches to reading instruction that include evidence-based methods at the word reading and reading comprehension levels.

Conducting functional analyses of reading performance is described as a viable method for testing the effectiveness of, or for determining, children's responsiveness to reading interventions. Included in each chapter are suggestion sections called "What can school psychologists and other educational consultants do?" The contents of these sections demonstrate how to put the information to practical use.

This book is not exhaustive of all there is to know about reading. We are learning more and more about the process of reading every day, so readers of this book are strongly encouraged to stay informed on current research and literature about reading. My hope is that this book contains important tools for school psychologists and other professionals to use as a foundation in their consultations.

SECTION ONE

Understanding Reading Development

This section consists of three chapters. Chapter 1, "How Children Emerge in Literacy," focuses on the requisite skills to help children become fluent readers. This chapter is designed to provide school psychologists and other consultants with knowledge about the precursors of literacy and the stages of literacy development so they can be aware of general patterns and the developmental progression of literacy skills. Understanding the stages of literacy development will help school psychologists and other consultants realize that virtually all children (including those with identified reading problems) develop reading and spelling in the same way. They also will understand why children read or spell the way they do, rather than automatically attributing children's difficulties to neurological abnormalities. Furthermore, this knowledge will help consultants interact more effectively with parents, teachers, and other interested stakeholders who raise questions concerning their child's developmental progression in becoming a fluent reader.

Many children may appear to have neurological abnormalities because of limited perceptual skills, when in reality they have not had opportunities or not been taught to read. Chapter 2, "Environmental Factors and Other Characteristics of Children Who Face Challenges in Becoming Literate," describes external factors that contribute to reading problems, such as poor instruction at school and limited experiences at home. This chapter describes characteristics of diverse types of children with reading problems.

Chapter 3, "Assessment of Reading Performance That Is Linked to Targeting Reading Interventions," presents an assessment process and tools to measure specific reading skills that are used to target appropriate interventions. Specifically, chapter 3 describes an assessment process that uses various data-gathering tools for deciding which types of reading interventions are appropriate to implement.

Chapter 1

How Children Emerge in Literacy

Dr. Smith says he does not remember how he learned to read;
he thought it seemed to have occurred naturally, like eating.
Why can't he recall?

Emergent literacy is a term coined by Marie Clay (1966) that refers to the beginnings of literacy or the process of becoming literate. Children begin to develop the precursors of literacy long before they walk into a classroom at school. Many of us cannot recall when or how we learned to read. For many of us, our memories do not take us back to a time before we began reading, so it is difficult to describe, even from our own experiences, the path to becoming a reader.

The majority of school psychologists and others working in a consultant role (with the exception of reading specialists) know very little about how reading develops and therefore cannot answer many questions regarding developmental expectations of children at various ages and grade levels. School psychologists, in particular, are expected to have a strong understanding about child development and human behavior, and they are likely to be approached about developmental and behavioral issues that are academically related. This chapter is primarily intended to provide school psychologists and other consultants with an understanding of how reading typically develops. Precursors of reading development such as oral language, vocabulary, and concepts about print are discussed; critical component skills and how they are connected are described in detail. These include phonemic awareness, alphabetic principle, phonological decoding, and orthographic processing, followed by oral reading development, reading fluency, reading vocabulary, and reading comprehension. Instruction on how to teach these skills effectively is presented in section 2 of this book.

LANGUAGE DEVELOPMENT

Miss Jones, a preschool teacher, was amazed how well Julio, a three-year-old boy, was able to predict what was going to happen next in a mystery story she was reading to the children. How might this happen?

Language development is one of the most critical precursors to developing literacy skills with ease. Many practitioners view oral language as a naturally developing skill and reading as a skill that needs to be taught. Certainly, reading is a skill that needs to be taught, but so does oral language, in a sense, because it does not develop as naturally as one may envision. Many educators would agree that language development begins in the home during instances when children have the opportunities to observe, listen, and use language to communicate with others and to receive communication from others. Language is most likely to develop through verbal interactions between caregivers (parents) and their children. Quality, as well as quantity, of verbal interactions is critical. These interactions establish the foundation ("background knowledge") on which children can build.

Quality of verbal interactions in the home refers to the types of dialogues that occur between parents or caregivers and their children. Many types of verbal interactions occur between parents and children, but those that help children reason and form verbal relationships about events or activities are considered to be *rich* or high-quality types of interactions (Nelson, 1996). High-quality verbal parent-to-child interactions include asking children questions that encourage an elaborate response or one that is beyond a *yes* or *no* response. Encouraging children to share in detail their own memories about an event such as a visit to the zoo or a vacation, or how they made an object with blocks or helped make cookies, would be considered eliciting high-quality verbal interactions (Nelson, 1996). Often, as children attempt to interact about a past trip or how they made something, they may need prompting to remember an event that occurred on their trip or a step in making an object. When parents prompt children in this manner, they are helping their children reason and organize information.

High-quality verbal interactions can also occur during an activity that the parents and their child are currently doing together. For instance, putting a puzzle together can be a rich opportunity to model and elicit oral language. Before beginning to put the puzzle together, parents can vocalize a strategy for arranging the pieces or plan to work from the outside to the inside; better yet, they can ask the child for ideas on how to proceed with the task. During the activity, parents can verbalize their thinking about a puzzle piece and why they think it may fit with another piece and then encourage the child to verbalize his or her thinking while working on putting the pieces together.

Storytelling and storybook reading are two high-quality activities that many young children repeatedly enjoy. During these activities, children can discover the meanings of words, label pictures, make predictions, and form cause-and-effect relationships. Guiding children through a story by asking questions and providing them with feedback and then encouraging extensions on their responses stimulate high-quality verbal interactions (Thomas, 1985).

In general, high-quality verbal interactions not only build vocabulary and sentence formation skills but also foster analytical and synthetic reasoning skills as well as the use of language as a tool for problem solving. These types of rich dialogues were found to contribute to children's linguistic and cognitive growth (Nelson, 1996).

The quantity of verbal interactions is also very important. In fact, Hart and Risley (1995) reported that children who resided in families that listened and talked to one another frequently had higher linguistic and vocabulary skills than children who engaged in limited verbal communications. These differences particularly occurred between social classes (Alexander, Entwisle, & Olson, 2001). Parents who had professional careers and high socioeconomic status tended to listen and talk to their children more frequently and engage in more high-quality verbal interactions than parents who had working-class jobs or parents who were on welfare. Thus, the children from professional families entered school knowing more than double the number of vocabulary words that children from working-class and welfare families did (Graves & Slater, 1987; Hart & Risley, 1995).

Language gaps between children residing in low socioeconomic households and those residing in high socioeconomic households continue into formal school years despite exposures and opportunities to similar types of instruction. This finding was very prevalent in a study conducted by Entwisle, Alexander, and Olson (1997). These researchers found that children who resided in middle-class families were likely to engage in more enriching activities outside of school during weekends and vacation times than children residing in low-income families. Enriching activities included going to the library, museums, historical sites such as national monuments, and family vacations. These findings should be interpreted with caution, as this does not necessarily mean that children from low socioeconomic families speak less than children from high socioeconomic families. Children from working-class and welfare families should not automatically be classified as poor readers, and children from professional families should not automatically be classified as proficient readers. Much of the vocabulary found in books at the preprimer and primer levels are words that are in most all children's oral language repertoires despite their parents' socioeconomic status (McCormick, 2003).

Structures of Spoken Language

The structures of spoken language are learned at very early ages even though children may not yet be able to identify parts of speech (Bloom, Barss, Nicol, & Conway, 1994). Through frequent verbal interactions, children begin to imitate their parents' speech and eventually learn syntax (sentence structure) and semantics (meaning; Golinkoff & Hirsch-Pasek, 1995). Very young children may say a phrase or a sentence that is often stated by their parents, such as "Mommy go bye-bye." They listen to how language is arranged in a certain way so that it makes sense or conveys statements that are easily understood.

This is evident as children's sentence length grows from two words to four, and so on. As children continue to become linguistically sophisticated, their spoken language reflects a more complex and wider range of grammatical structures. Chaney (1992) found that syntactic and semantic language skills were predictors of performance in phonological skills for a sample of preschoolers.

Pragmatics of Language

Young children also learn the various uses of language or the pragmatics of language (Ninio & Snow, 1996). Very young children soon learn to use their words as a means to communicate their needs or make requests instead of crying, babbling, or gesturing. They also begin to learn how adults communicate with each other during conversational situations, such as at the dinner table. They soon realize that language is used in genres such as storytelling or storybook reading time. Young children not only discover the pragmatics of language but also begin to think about and manipulate language, in a process of developing *metalinguistic skills*.

Language and Reading

Having adequate language skills, including vocabulary, can help children read and comprehend text with more ease when they encounter printed words (de Jong & Leseman, 2001; Roth, Speece, & Cooper, 2002). Learning how to read does not come naturally to children, but they will encounter the task with more ease if they can match printed words and their meanings to words and meanings they have in their oral language repertoires (McCormick, 2003). Knowledge of oral language provides a way for children to self-check words they are reading and determine if they sound syntactically or semantically correct. Oral language in this context does not necessarily refer to children who are observed to talk aloud often. Some children are quiet by nature and engage in private speech and sub-vocalizations at significantly higher rates than overt vocalizations.

Acquiring language is not a guarantee that children will become proficient readers, even though language correlates significantly with reading performance (Scarborough, 1998). Written language and oral language structures differ with regard to the way sentence patterns are constructed. This is one of the reasons children should listen to storybooks being read to them (McCormick, 2003). Reading aloud is a very important activity if you want to expose children through oral language to the way sentence patterns are constructed in written language before children actually read the printed words in a book.

CRITICAL COMPONENT SKILLS

Reading is a complex activity involving several component skills (National Reading Panel, 2000). Research has shown that children who do not learn basic early component skills of reading are likely to be at a disadvantage during their formal schooling years and beyond (Moats, 1999). Each of these skills is necessary but alone is not sufficient to allow a child to become a proficient reader. The goal of reading is to move from learning to read to reading to learn. Several of the component skills discussed in this section need to be automatized or appropriated if learners are to use reading as a tool for obtaining information or as a recreational activity that brings them pleasure and entertainment.

Concepts About Print

While watching a video in which he was reading a book to his nine-month-old daughter as they sat on the couch, Sam reported that he noticed his infant daughter's head tilted and her eyes moved from left to right.
Can infants read?

Although a picture may be worth a thousand words, it is important that children eventually realize that it is printed words, not pictures, that reveal a message. When children have concepts about print, it means that they are able to distinguish words from pictures, know that a book has a front and a back, know that books are read right side up, and know that printed words across a page in a book are read from left to right and top to bottom (Clay, 1993). Children develop concepts about print very early, often at home before they enter formal schooling (Morrow & Young, 1997). According to a report provided by the National Research Council (edited by Snow, Burns, & Griffin, 1998), children from birth through three years of age begin to develop concepts about print as they recognize specific books by the cover, label pictured objects in books, and pretend to read books.

It is not the presence of the print materials that is most critical, although that is important. Rather, it is the quantity and quality of interactions with print that shape early reading development (Mason & Allen, 1986). Concepts about print are best learned through interactions with parents or caregivers during routine storybook reading time. This is the time when parents demonstrate how to hold a book, how to turn pages, and how to read words from left to right, often by running their index finger across the page in a left to right sweeping motion as they read the words. Children are also prompted to put their fingers on a page and point to the words on a page rather than the pictures. Concepts about print can be taught during playtime or in a preschool classroom through make-believe play activities such as working in a restaurant as a waiter taking orders or as a customer reading and ordering from the menu or pretend-working in a post office where letters are addressed and stamped. These types of activities were found to be very effective in helping preschoolers gain concepts about print (Neuman & Roskos, 1992).

Phonological Awareness

Sally can identify beginning and ending sounds, but she has difficulty identifying the middle sounds in spoken words.
What does this mean?

The acquisition of phonological awareness skills plays a primary role later in recognizing and comprehending printed text (Torgesen & Mathes, 2000). Phonological awareness is alertness to the sounds in spoken language. It is also the operation and manipulation of sounds in spoken words. Numerous studies have revealed that phonological awareness, rather than intellectual ability, is a better predictor of word reading performance for children in the early primary grades (e.g., Share, McGee, & Silva, 1989; Siegel, 1988; Stanovich, Cunningham, & Freeman, 1984; Stanovich & Siegel, 1994; Vellutino, Scanlon, & Lyon, 2000). Explicit training in phonological awareness during the preschool and kindergarten years may also have the potential to mediate the effects of poverty (Kaplan & Walpole, 2005).

According to Lundberg, Frost, and Peterson (1988), phonological awareness involves the following developmental progression of skills: (1) rhyming, especially the production of rhymes, (2) hearing individual syllables in words, (3) hearing initial sounds of words, and (4) hearing sounds within words. Rhyme production may involve having children co-construct a jingle or a poem by taking turns with their parents or teachers creating a phrase that rhymes with the previous phrase. Eventually, young children will feel comfortable producing their own rhymes without assistance from others. Children can learn to attend to individual syllables in words by clapping or counting the syllables. Children can attend to initial sounds in words by being shown a picture of an object and saying the word it represents, followed by its beginning sound. In that activity, three additional pictures are presented. One of the pictures depicts an object with the same beginning sound as the first picture presented. Children can circle, point to, or say the word of the picture that has the same beginning sound as the first picture presented. The same activity can be used to help children attend to ending sounds in words.

Learning to hear sounds within words can be presented through an oddity task or odd-one-out task. Children may be presented with the words sit, fit, kit, and cat and asked to choose one that sounds different from the others. Generally, children attend to beginning and ending sounds before attending to middle sounds during phonological awareness exercises.

According to Lane, Pullen, Eisele, and Jordan (2002), there are four levels of phonological awareness development: (1) Young children first become aware that speech flow is a collection of individual words. (2) Young children distinguish syllables in spoken words followed by onset and rime activities (intrasyllabic level). For instance, the onset may be the consonant sound that precedes the vowel, such as the /c/ in the word *cat*. The rime is the rest of the word, such as /at/ in the word *cat*. This is considered to be a rather sophisticated phonological awareness skill because tasks that require onset-rime analysis involve segmentation of syllables. (3) The final level is the phoneme level, which is most commonly referred to as phonemic awareness and is considered to be the most sophisticated level.

Phonemic awareness is one of the most important components of phonological awareness because it has been found to be a critical precursor skill to successful reading and spelling performance (Ball & Blachman, 1991; Bentin & Leshem, 1993; Byrne & Fielding-Barnsley, 1991; Griffith, 1991; Hatcher, Hulme, & Ellis, 1994; Juel, 1988; Stahl & Murray,

1994; Tangel & Blachman, 1992). Phonemic awareness is a more specific skill that requires attention to and manipulation of *individual* sounds of spoken words. A phoneme is the smallest unit of sound (an individual sound) in a word. The English language contains approximately forty-one phonemes.

Daly, Chafouleas, and Skinner (2005) provide a hierarchy of phonemic awareness skills or skills that, more specifically, involve the manipulation of individual sounds in words. The first skill in their hierarchy of skills is *alliteration*. This skill involves having the child identify and say the first sound in a word, such as saying /c/ for the word *cat*, and identifying words that have the same first sound, such as categorizing *cap* with *cat* when the words *sun, cap,* and *dog* are presented. The next skill is *blending*, which consists of blending the individual sounds of a word to make a whole word, such as /c-a-t/ to form the word *cat*. Blending is followed by the child segmenting the sounds of a word by clapping three times as each sound in the word /c-a-t/ is slowly articulated, or by saying each of the individual sounds heard in the word *cat*.

The final skills in the developmental progression involve deleting, substituting, and reversing individual sounds in words to make new words. When the word *cat* is articulated, children are asked to say the new word when the /c/ sound "walks away" and when the /b/ sound "comes over to stand" in the /c/ place, as in *bat*. Children may also reverse the sounds in the word *bat* to form another word, *tab*, and add sounds to a word, such as adding /s/ to the word *tab* to form the word *stab*. Among the phonological awareness skills, Nation and Hulme (1997) found that phoneme segmentation skills were the best predictors of word reading performance for a sample of first graders.

Phonemic awareness has been strongly related to phonological memory, especially at the early ages (Wagner, Torgesen, Laughon, Simmons, & Rashotte, 1993). According to Torgesen (1988), phonological memory (sometimes called *memory span*) is a process by which individuals store phonological codes in their working or short-term memory. Gathercole and Baddeley (1990) found that deficits in phonological memory did not affect elementary school-age children's ability to speak and read known words but did affect their ability to speak and read words that were unknown to them. Phonological memory becomes more crucial as children grow older and confront new complex words such as multisyllabic words. If children are unable to store all of the sounds or chunks of sounds in their immediate memories, they may have difficulty blending all of the sounds to form a whole word. Thus, phonological memory is a characteristic that distinguishes good readers from poor readers (Muter & Snowling, 1998; Swanson, 1992; Torgesen, 1988; Vellutino et al., 1996).

Whereas phonological memory involves the storage of phonological codes, *rapid naming* refers to the efficient retrieval of that phonological information (McDougall, Hulme, Ellis, & Monk, 1994). In other words, rapid naming is rapidly accessing phonological codes to speak and read fluently. Rapid naming tasks are timed and typically consist of naming objects, digits, letters, or words quickly or automatically. Children experienced the greatest difficulty learning to read if they exhibited a combination of limited rapid naming and phonological awareness skills (Wolf & Bowers, 1999; Bowers & Wolf, 1993). Some investigations have revealed correlations between rapid naming and phonological awareness, letter-name knowledge, and very basic decoding skills (Compton, 2003). Others have found significant relationships between rapid naming and orthographic and reading comprehension skills (Bowers, 1995; Cutting & Denkla, 2001; Manis, Doi, & Bhadha, 2000). Although investigations have reported a relationship between rapid naming and other early literacy skills, some researchers have found that the relationship is stronger for intermediate graders than it is for primary graders (Kirby, Pfeiffer, & Parrila, 2000).

Orthographic Knowledge

Johnny, a beginning kindergartner, can name all the letters in the alphabet but does not know the sounds that all the letters make. Is this "normal"?

Orthographic knowledge involves *lexical processing* of words, which means analyzing the visual or graphic structures of letters and words and involves storing these lexical features in memory (Olson, Forsberg, Wise, & Rack, 1994). At least as early as three years of age, children begin attending to letters in names, particularly their own name (Snow, Burns, & Griffin, 1998). Knowing about letters (*graphemes*) and noting letter sequences in words require orthographic skills (Ehri, 1991).

Many young children (four to five years old) may be able to name the letters of the alphabet, either by reciting the alphabet orally or by singing the alphabet song or by looking at the printed symbols and naming the letters. In some cases, even three-year-olds have been known to name ten letters of the alphabet (Snow et al., 1998). Typically, children are able to do this before they are able to identify the sounds that the letters represent (Worden & Boettcher, 1990). Letter naming, especially letter-naming fluency, has been found to be related to early reading skills (Johnston, Anderson, & Holligan, 1996), although some claim that the relationship between letter-naming training and word recognition acquisition is not as strong as the relationship between phoneme awareness and word recognition acquisition (e.g., Allor, 2002; Ball & Blachman, 1991; McBride-Chang, 1999). However, some earlier investigations reported that training programs that combined phonemic awareness exercises, such as phoneme segmentation, with letter-shape instruction produced greater outcomes in early reading acquisition skills than general language skills instruction (Bentin & Leshem, 1993). Knowledge of letter names influences children's early attempts to write words (Treiman & Tincoff, 1997).

In their later development of orthographic features of language, children (particularly those in the primary grades) begin to note letter sequences or spelling patterns in words and how combinations or patterns of letters are strung together and represent certain sounds. For instance, when two letters that represent vowel sounds follow one another in the middle of a word such as in the words *meat* and *gait*, the sound of the first letter representing the vowel sound is heard rather than the subsequent letter. For the word *meat*, the long /e/

sound is heard, and the long /a/ sound is heard for the word *gait*. These types of spelling patterns found in words make it possible for words to be learned by analogy and automatically (McCormick, 2003). For instance, once a learner knows how to read the words *main*, *pain*, and *rain*, they are likely to learn how to read the word *stain* with much ease and with little assistance. Recalling orthographic features of words can be challenging when words sound alike but are spelled differently, such as *pane* and *pain*. Orthographic knowledge of words also plays a role in obtaining morphemic (meaning) units of words such as prefixes and suffixes (Frith, 1985; Nagy, Berninger, Abbot, Vaughan, & Vermeulen, 2003).

Alphabetic Principle

In a seminal book about beginning reading, Adams (1990) proclaims that acquiring phonemic awareness and letter-naming skills eases one's way to understanding the alphabetic principle. According to Torgesen and Mathes (2000), phonemic awareness helps children understand the alphabetic principle, helps children become aware of the regular ways letters represent sounds, and makes it possible to identify words in context even if they can only be partially sounded out.

The *alphabetic principle* refers to knowing that there is an association between letters and sounds or that there are letter-sound relations. One way to learn letter-sound relations is by having children read alphabet books that contain printed upper- and lowercase letters, pictures, and words that represent the sounds of the respective featured letters. For instance, to understand that /b/ is for *bear*, children need to understand that the first sound in bear is /b/. Some experts have suggested that lowercase letters should be taught first because the majority of words in reading text are printed in lowercase letters (Carnine, Silbert, Kame'enui, & Tarver, 2004). This may be the case for children who have limited prerequisite literacy skills, and learning lowercase letters may quickly lead to engaging in printed text. Children who can make approximately forty letter-sound correspondences in one minute by the end of kindergarten are at an advantage for beginning reading instruction when they enter first grade (Casey & Howe, 2002). Thus, word reading strategies begin to develop when children begin to make connections between phonological and orthographic features of language. Blachman, Tangel, Ball, Black, and McGraw (1999) found that kindergarten children who received a combination of phonemic awareness, letter-naming, and letter-sound training outperformed their peers (control group) in reading phonetically regular words, reading pseudowords, and spelling basic words.

Phonological Recoding and Decoding

Mr. Jones reported that Jamie, a first grader, had an "Aha" moment when he read the word dog for the first time and said, "Oh, I know this word. I have a pet dog." Why did Jamie say this?

When children encounter printed words and attempt to read the words, they go through a process of *phonological recoding*, which means they try to recode the printed word back to its oral representation (Share, 1995). Similarly, Vandervelden and Siegel (1997) defined phonological recoding as retrieving the pronunciation of a word in one's oral vocabulary when it is newly encountered in print through systematic relationships between letters and sounds. Essentially, the term *recoding* rather than *decoding* is used here to describe the process because children check to see if the word they are reading matches one in their speaking vocabulary repertoire (Daneman, 1991). This process is a reminder about the valuable connection between oral and written language.

Many of the basic words in print that first graders encounter are words with consonant-vowel-consonant patterns (CVC). These words often require a one-to-one letter-sound correspondence. Children are taught to sequentially decode these types of printed words by making one-to-one sequential letter–sound correspondences, such as blending the sounds of the letters c-u-p to produce the word *cup*. At more advanced levels, children hierarchically decode words by using letters in words to cue the sounds of other letters, such as using the letter "e" at the end of the word *cake* to cue them to make a long vowel sound for the letter "a" (McCormick, 2003).

Phonological coding involves applying the alphabetic principle, which is the linking of phonological and orthographic features of language. A reciprocal relationship likely exists between the development of spoken and written language. Awareness of sounds in spoken language aids in decoding written language, and developing written language skills such as reading and writing contributes to growth in oral language (Chase & Tallal, 1991). Perfetti, Beck, Bell, and Hughes (1987) discovered that children's growth in word reading skills strengthened their phonological awareness skills.

Word Reading

Tiffany paused when she came across a word that was unfamiliar to her and decided to use letter-sound correspondence strategies to figure out how to read it.
Is this word recognition or word identification?

Word reading is a more general term that encompasses word recognition and word identification skills. Often, the terms *word recognition* and *word identification* are used synonymously. McCormick (2003) provides a clear distinction between these two terms. She defines word recognition as the instant recall of words or reading of words by sight. Word identification refers to the instances when the reader needs to access one or more strategies to aid in reading a word. Children who are proficient at the use of strategy almost make it seem as if they are reading the words effortlessly, whereas children who have had little experience with strategy use appear to exert much effort in figuring out how to read a word.

Ehri and McCormick (1998) postulated the following phases of word learning: (1) prealphabetic, (2) partial alphabetic, (3) full alphabetic, (4) consolidated alphabetic, and (5) automatic. In the prealphabetic stage, children have knowledge of logographic features (word graphic features), and they employ these features to read words. For instance, they may recognize a word by its shape or length. They do not tend to recognize many words in context-free situations. Children in this stage do not make letter-sound associations; however, they may be able to remember and read words that they have been exposed to repeatedly. In the partial alphabetic stage, children are able to recognize more words in isolation (context-free situations) as they use more letter cues to recognize words. Some analytical skills are applied, such as breaking down words into letters and using beginning and ending sounds to recognize words; however, most words are read by sight. In the next stage (full alphabetic), students begin to learn and use more letter-sound associations to read words. Children may be observed to point to each letter of a word and decode a word very slowly using a one-to-one correspondence between letters and sounds. Later, they are able to decode words more quickly. In this stage, children learn many more words than in previous stages.

In the consolidated alphabetic stage, children begin to recognize words by analogy, especially words that share common spelling and sound patterns (sometimes referred to as phonograms or *word family* words). For example, children are able to read the word *hike* because they already know how to read the words *bike* and *like*. Familiar spelling-pattern units in words, such as those that end in "ip," are easily pronounced (e.g., *sip*, *dip*, and *zip*), which makes bigger words, such as *skip* or *zipper*, more manageable (less overwhelming) to decode. Reading a significantly greater number of words and reading them more fluently are evident in this phase.

The final phase of word reading is the automatic phase. Most all words are recognized by sight or effortlessly. Readers have a variety of strategies that they systematically apply when reading words that are unfamiliar. When children learn to read several words, they are likely to read more words at increasingly higher rates. This phenomenon is what Stanovich (1986) called the "Matthew effects of reading" (good readers get better and poor readers get poorer).

It is important that children reach the automatic stage of word reading so that less of their cognitive effort is spent figuring out how to read print. Instead, their effort is spent obtaining meaning from print. Learning to read, in a sense, is a complex process, because words may be presented in structurally diverse ways in various genres or types of literature; therefore, it is important that children reach a stage at which they are reading to learn. This is especially critical during formal schooling, in which reading is required to obtain information across all academic content areas. Moreover, reading skills have become more critical beyond formal schooling years as society has advanced technologically.

Word reading and spelling develop closely together. Zutell (1998) describes five stages of spelling development: preliterate, phonetic or letter-name, transitional, syllable juncture spelling, and conventional spelling. The first stage is called the preliterate stage because children initially scribble. In this stage, they do not know all the names of letters and do not know any letter-sound relationships. Later in this stage, children begin to write a letter or letters that represent a sound or word. For instance, children may write the letter that their name begins with to represent their entire name or they may spell a word using three letters even though it is spelled using more letters. For instance, they may spell the word teacher as "ter." In stage two, the phonetic or letter-name stage, children can spell words using appropriate letter-sound associations although they still make errors, such as spelling "skipt" for skipped. Children then move on to a third stage, the transitional stage, when they often spell words using medial vowels and produce correct inflectional endings (e.g., "ed," "ing"). In stage four, syllable juncture spelling, children can spell a large number of single and multisyllabic words with high-frequency spelling patterns but still have difficulty with some complex doubled and unstressed vowels in polysyllabic words. Stage five is the conventional spelling stage. Children at this stage can correctly spell most words with confusing patterns, especially if they have had adequate exposure to the words. It is natural for children to invent the spellings of words when they are beginning to attempt to write words. However, it is important for children to eventually learn to spell conventionally so they may be able to effectively communicate in written form.

Passage Reading

Before children engage in passage reading, they engage in storybook reading with their parents, caregivers, or preschool teachers. From many observations of very young children, Sulzby (1985) generated developmental stages of how children's skills emerge in storybook reading. Beginning at about two to three years of age and continuing, children progress in their storybook reading skills by initially attending to pictures without forming stories yet, and then by attending to pictures and spontaneously forming oral stories. Soon, children attend to pictures, and their storytelling fluctuates from spontaneous storytelling to storytelling that appears as if they are reading text but they are not actually reading print yet. Children move from attending to pictures and sounding as if they are reading to attending to print and actually reading text (Sulzby, 1985).

Passage reading is important and should be included in primary grade instruction. Opportunities to practice reading words in context such as stories help children apply their word identification and recognition skills as well as their comprehension skills (Carnine et al., 2004).

Fluency

Jerome reads quickly but his voice sounds monotone.
Is Jerome a fluent reader?

The skill of reading fluency is critical to increasing the rate at which text is translated into spoken language (Torgesen, Rashotte, Alexander, Alexander, & MacPhee, 2003). Carnine et al. (2004) distinguished between the terms *automaticity* and *fluency*. They indicated that automaticity refers to reading words in isolation very swiftly and without much effort. They further stated that one cannot assume that if children read words automatically in isolation, they will be able to read words in a passage accurately and quickly. Nevertheless, increasing word recognition accuracy places children in a better position to read passages fluently. Fluency refers to reading words in passages in a flowing, accurate, quick, and expressive manner. Reading with expression (*prosody*) means exhibiting variations in pitch, pausing between sentences, stressing syllables, and using intonation that reflects the statements in the text (Hudson, Lane, & Pullen, 2005). Fluent readers can read an average of at least seventy-five to one hundred words per minute accurately, with three to five errors on grade-level passage text (Shinn, 1989).

Carnine et al. (2004) suggested that fluency exercises on oral reading passages should be incorporated in daily lessons until children read approximately 135 words per minute with 97 percent accuracy using fourth-grade reading materials. Having no errors or minimal errors in reading is critical to gaining meaning from text (National Center for Educational Statistics, 2002). Children who do not read fluently often read passages very slowly, laboring over many words one by one. Reading fluency is a good predictor of reading comprehension performance (National Reading Panel, 2000; Rasinski, 1990). Fluency not only contributes to better comprehension of text but also may eliminate frustration caused by working slowly and needing more time to accomplish assignments, especially in the intermediate grades (Carnine et al., 2004).

Reading Vocabulary and Comprehension

When Carisa began to read the new story of the week, she told her teacher that she remembered reading about trains and how they operated in the Polar Express *book.*
What is Carisa doing?

Knowing the meanings of words and concepts and comprehending text are as critical as knowing how to recognize words and read them fluently. Reading vocabulary and comprehension are very much related to receptive and expressive language knowledge and skills. A reciprocal relationship exists between oral and written language growth. An adequate language base (e.g., vocabulary) eases children's way into written text. Engaging in reading and writing activities enhances children's language knowledge and skills (e.g., increasing vocabulary). Children use language skills when, according to McCormick (2003), they attend to the propositions or the smallest units of text information that can be tested as true or false and stand separately when children attempt to comprehend them. Children also activate their prior knowledge and experiences, or schemata, when the contents of the text are familiar. Intertextuality is observed when children make connections between new textual information and textual information that they read in the past (Short, 1992). Therefore, comprehending text is a complex skill because it involves understanding text structure, making inferences, knowing word meanings, and relating sentences, paragraphs, and so forth to each other (Randi, Grigorenko, & Sternberg, 2005).

WHAT CAN SCHOOL PSYCHOLOGISTS AND OTHER EDUCATIONAL CONSULTANTS DO?

1. While observing students, attend to where they are developmentally with regard to prereading and reading skills.
2. Dispel unsupported myths about learning how to read.
3. Help educators incorporate the teaching of critical component prereading and reading skills in their daily lessons.
4. Help educators incorporate basic as well as higher-order reading skills according to individual students' needs.
5. Help educators realize the importance of teaching to mastery and fluency.
6. Give educators an opportunity to share their instructional reading lessons and materials and help them engage in continuous enhancement activities so that lessons and materials are conducive to meeting students' needs.

SUMMARY POINTS

- Language development is related to reading development.
- High-quality verbal interaction between caregivers and children refers to helping children describe events, engage in verbal problem-solving, and form cause-effect relationships.
- *Quantity of verbal interactions* refers to how frequently caregivers listen and talk to their children.
- Acquisition of syntactic, semantic, and pragmatic elements of oral language eases children's path to becoming literate.
- Concepts about reading print can be learned very early, especially during storybook time, when caregivers demonstrate how to hold a book, turn pages, and read words from left to right.
- *Phonemic awareness* is the alertness to and manipulation of sounds in spoken language, including segmenting and blending of sounds.
- *Orthographic knowledge* refers to an awareness of how letters are sequenced in words (spelling patterns).
- *Alphabetic principle* refers to the knowledge that a relationship exists between letters and sounds. For instance, when children encounter printed words, they recode that word back to its oral representation.
- *Fluency* includes accuracy, speed, and prosody.
- Reading comprehension involves understanding text structure, making inferences, knowing word meanings, and relating sentences and paragraphs to each other.

QUESTIONS FOR DISCUSSION

1. How do oral language skills, conception of ideas expressed in print, and phonological awareness play a part in reading development?

2. What are the differences between phonological recoding and phonological decoding?
3. Distinguish between word recognition and word identification.
4. Why does word recognition promote reading fluency and reading comprehension?
5. How might oral language skills, conception of ideas expressed in print, and phonological awareness also play a part in spelling and writing development?

REFERENCES

Adams, M. J. (1990). *Beginning to Read: Thinking and Learning about Print.* Cambridge, MA: MIT Press.

Alexander, K. L., Entwisle, D. R., & Olson, L. S. (2001). Schools, achievement, and inequality: A seasonal perspective. *Educational Evaluation and Policy Analysis, 23,* 171–191.

Allor, J. H. (2002). The relationship of phoneme awareness and rapid naming to reading development. *Learning Disability Quarterly, 25,* 47–58.

Ball, E., & Blachman, B. (1991). Does phonemic awareness training in kindergarten make a difference in early word recognition and developmental spelling? *Reading Research Quarterly, 26,* 49–66.

Bentin, S., & Leshem, H. (1993). On the interaction between phonological awareness and reading acquisition: It's a two-way street. *Annals of Dyslexia, 43,* 125–148.

Blachman, B. A., Tangel, D. M., Ball, E. W., Black, R., & McGraw, C. K. (1999). Developing phonological awareness and word recognition skills: A two-year intervention with low-income, inner city children. *Reading and Writing: An Interdisciplinary Journal, 11,* 239–273.

Bloom, P., Barss, A., Nicol, J., & Conway, L. (1994). Children's knowledge of binding and coreference: Evidence from spontaneous speech. *Language, 70,* 53–71.

Bowers, P. G. (1995). Tracing symbol naming speed's unique contributions to reading disabilities over time. *Reading and Writing: An Interdisciplinary Journal, 7,* 189–216.

Bowers, P. G., & Wolf, M. (1993). Theoretical links between naming speed, precise timing mechanisms, and orthographic skill in dyslexia. *Reading and Writing: An Interdisciplinary Journal, 5,* 69–85.

Byrne, B., & Fielding-Barnsley, R. (1991). Evaluation of a program to teach phonemic awareness to young children. *Journal of Educational Psychology, 83,* 451–455.

Carnine, D. W., Silbert, J., Kame'enui, E. J., & Tarver, S. G. (Eds.). (2004). *Direct instruction reading.* (4th ed.) Upper Saddle River, NJ: Pearson.

Casey, A., & Howe, K. (2002). Best practices in early literacy skills. In A. Thomas & J. Grimes (Eds.), *Best Practices in School Psychology IV*. Bethesda, MD: National Association of School Psychologists.

Chaney, C. (1992). Language development, metalinguistic skills, and print awareness in 3-year-old children. *Applied Psycholinguistics, 13,* 485–514.

Chase, C. H., & Tallal, P. (1991). Cognitive models of developmental reading disorders. In J. Orbrutz & G. W. Hynd (Eds.), *Neuropsychological Foundations of Learning Disabilities* (pp. 199–240). San Diego, CA: Academic Press.

Clay, M. (1966). Emergent reading behavior. Unpublished doctoral dissertation, University of Auckland, New Zealand.

Clay, M. (1993). *Reading Recovery: A Guidebook for Teachers in Training.* Portsmouth, NH: Heinemann.

Compton, D. L. (2003). Modeling the relationship between growth in rapid naming speed and growth in decoding skill in first-grade children. *Journal of Educational Psychology, 95,* 225–239.

Cutting, L. E., & Denkla, M. B. (2001). The relationship of rapid serial naming and word reading in normally developing readers: An exploratory model. *Reading and Writing: An Interdisciplinary Journal, 14,* 673–705.

Daly, E. J., III, Chafouleas, S., & Skinner, C. H. (2005). *Interventions for Reading Problems: Designing and Evaluating Effective Strategies.* New York: Guilford Press.

Daneman, M. (1991). Individual differences in reading skills. In R. Barr, M. L. Kamil, P. Mosenthal, & P. D. Pearson (Eds.), *Handbook of Reading Research* (Vol. 11, pp. 512–538). New York: Longman.

de Jong, P. F., & Leseman, P. M. (2001). Lasting effects of home literacy on reading achievement in school. *Journal of School Psychology, 39,* 389–414.

Ehri, L. C. (1991). Development of the ability to read words. In R. Barr, M. L. Kamil, P. B. Mosenthal, & P. D. Pearson (Eds.), *Handbook of Reading Research* (Vol. 11, pp. 383–417). New York: Longman.

Ehri, L. C., & McCormick, S. (1998). Phases of word learning: Implications for instruction with delayed and disabled readers. *Reading and Writing Quarterly, 14,* 135–163.

Entwisle, D., Alexander, K. L., & Olson, L. (1997). *Children, Schools, and Inequality.* Boulder, CO: Westview.

Frith, V. (1985). Beneath the surface of developmental dyslexia. In K. E. Patterson, J. C. Marshall & M. Coltheart (Eds.), *Surface Dyslexia* (pp. 301–330). London: Erlbaum.

Gathercole, S. E., & Baddeley, A. D. (1990). Phonological memory deficits in language disordered children: Is there a causal connection? *Journal of Memory and Language, 29,* 336–360.

Golinkoff, R. M., & Hirsch-Pasek, K. (1995). Reinterpreting children's sentence comprehension: Toward a new framework. In B. MacWhinney & P. Fletcher (Eds.), *Handbook of Child Language*. Oxford, U.K.: Blackwell.

Graves, M. F., & Slater, W. H. (1987, April). Development of reading vocabularies in rural disadvantaged students, intercity disadvantaged students, and middle class suburban students. Paper presented at AERA conference, Washington, D.C.

Griffith, P. (1991). Phonemic awareness helps first graders invent spellings and third graders remember correct spellings. *Journal of Reading Behavior, 23,* 215–233.

Hart, B., & Risley, T. R. (1995). *Meaningful Differences in the Everyday Experience of Young American Children*. Baltimore: Brookes.

Hatcher, P., Hulme, C., & Ellis, A. W. (1994). Ameliorating reading failure by integrating the teaching of reading and phonological skills: The phonological linkage hypothesis. *Child Development, 65,* 41–57.

Hudson, R. F., Lane, H. B., & Pullen, P. C. (2005). Reading fluency assessment and instruction: What, why, and how? *The Reading Teacher, 58,* 702–714.

Johnston, R. S., Anderson, M., & Holligan, C. (1996). Knowledge of the alphabet and explicit awareness of phonemes in prereaders: The nature of the relationship. *Reading and Writing: An Interdisciplinary Journal, 8,* 217–234.

Juel, C. (1988). Learning to read and write: A longitudinal study of 54 children from first through fourth grades. *Journal of Educational Psychology, 80,* 417–447.

Kaplan, D., & Walpole, S. (2005). A stage-sequential model of reading transitions: Evidence from the early childhood longitudinal study. *Journal of Educational Psychology, 97,* 551–563.

Kirby, J. R., Pfeiffer, S. L., & Parrila, R. K. (2000). Naming speed and phonological awareness as predictors of reading development. *Journal of Educational Psychology, 95,* 453–464.

Lane, H. B., Pullen, P. C., Eisele, M. R., & Jordan, L. (2002). Preventing reading failure: Phonological awareness assessment and instruction. *Preventing School Failure, 46,* 101–110.

Lundberg, I., Frost, J., & Peterson, O. P. (1988). Effects of an extensive program for stimulating phonological awareness in preschool children. *Reading Research Quarterly, 23*, 204–284.

Manis, F. R., Doi, L. M., & Bhadha, B. (2000). Naming speed, phonological awareness, and orthographic knowledge in second graders. *Journal of Learning Disabilities, 33*, 325–333.

Mason, J. M., & Allen, J. (1986). A review of emergent literacy with implications for research and practice in reading. In E. Z. Rothkopf (Ed.), *Review of Research in Education*. Washington, D.C.: American Educational Research Association.

McBride-Chang, C. (1999). The ABCs of the ABCs: The development of letter-name and letter-sound knowledge. *Merrill-Palmer Quarterly, 45*, 285–307.

McCormick, S. (Ed.). (2003). *Instructing Students Who Have Literacy Problems*. Upper Saddle River, NJ: Pearson.

McDougall, S., Hulme, C., Ellis, A., & Monk, A. (1994). Learning to read: The role of short-term memory and phonological skills. *Journal of Experimental Child Psychology, 58*, 112–133.

Moats, L. C. (1999). *Teaching Reading is Rocket Science: What Expert Teachers of Reading Should Know and be Able to Do*. New York: American Federation of Teachers.

Morrow, L., & Young, J. (1997). A family literacy program connecting school and home: Effects on attitude, motivation, and literacy achievement. *Journal of Educational Psychology, 89*, 736–742.

Muter, V., & Snowling, M. (1998). Concurrent and longitudinal predictors of reading: The role of metalinguistic and short-term memory skills. *Reading Research Quarterly, 33*, 320–337.

Nagy, W., Berninger, V., Abbot, R., Vaughan, K., & Vermeulen, K. (2003). Relationship of morphology and other language skills in at-risk second-grade readers and at-risk fourth-grade writers. *Journal of Educational Psychology, 95*, 730–742.

Nation, K., & Hulme, C. (1997). Phonemic segmentation, not onset-rime segmentation, predicts early reading and spelling skills. *Reading Research Quarterly, 32*, 154–167.

National Center for Educational Statistics. (2002). *National Assessment of Educational Progress*. Retrieved July 20, 2005 from www.nces.ed.gov

National Reading Panel. (2000). *Teaching Children to Read: An Evidence-Based Assessment of the Scientific Research Literature on Reading and its Implications for Reading*

Instruction. Washington, D.C.: NICH. Retrieved July 26, 2005 from www.nichd.nih.gov /publications/nrp/smallbook.htm

Nelson, K. (1996). *Language in Cognitive Development: The Emergence of the Mediated Mind.* New York: Cambridge University Press.

Neuman, S., & Roskos, K. (1992). Literacy objects as cultural tools: Effects on children's literacy behaviors in play. *Reading Research Quarterly, 27,* 203–225.

Ninio, A., & Snow, C. E. (1996). *Pragmatic Development.* Boulder, CO: Westview.

Olson, R., Forsberg, H., Wise, B., & Rack, J. (1994). Measurement of word recognition, orthographic, and phonological skills. In G. R. Lyon (Ed.), *Frames of Reference for the Assessment of Learning Disabilities. New Views on Measurement Issues* (pp. 243–277). Baltimore: Brookes.

Perfetti, C., Beck, L., Bell, L., & Hughes, C. (1987). Children's reading and development of phonological awareness. *Merrill-Palmer Quarterly, 33,* 39–75.

Randi, J., Grigorenko, E. L., & Sternberg, R. J. (2005). Revisiting definitions of reading comprehension: Just what is reading comprehension anyway? In S. E. Israel, C. C. Block, K. L. Bauserman, & K. Kinnucan-Welsch (Eds.), *Metacognition in Literacy Learning: Theory, Assessment, Instruction, and Professional Development* (pp. 19–40). Mahwah, NJ: Erlbaum.

Rasinski, T. (1990). Effects of repeated reading and listening while reading on reading fluency. *Journal of Educational Research, 83,* 147–150.

Roth, F. P., Speece, D. L., & Cooper, D. H. (2002). A longitudinal analysis of the connection between oral language and early reading. *Journal of Educational Research, 95,* 259–272.

Scarborough, H. S. (1998). Early identification of children at risk for reading disabilities: Phonological awareness and some other promising predictors. In B. K. Shapiro, P. J. Accardo, & A. J. Capute (Eds.), *Specific Reading Disability: A View of the Spectrum* (pp. 77–121). Timonium, MD: York Press.

Share, D. L. (1995). Phonological recoding and self-teaching: Sine qua non of reading acquisition. *Cognition, 55,* 151–218.

Share, D. L., McGee, R., & Silva, P. A. (1989). IQ and reading progress: A test of the capacity notion of IQ. *Journal of the American Academy of Child and Adolescent Psychiatry, 28,* 97–100.

Shinn, M. R. (Ed.). (1989). *Curriculum-Based Measurement: Assessing Special Children.* New York: Guilford Press.

Short, K. G. (1992). Intertextuality: Searching for patterns that connect. In C. K. Kinzer & D. J. Leu (Eds.), *Literacy Research, Theory, and Practice: Views from Many Perspectives* (pp. 187–197). Chicago: National Reading Conference.

Siegel, L. S. (1988). Evidence that IQ scores are irrelevant to the definition and analysis of reading disability. *Canadian Journal of Psychology, 42,* 201–215.

Snow, C. E., Burns, S., & Griffin, P. (1998). *Preventing Reading Difficulties in Young Children.* Washington, D.C.: National Academy Press.

Stanovich, K. E. (1986). Matthew effects on reading: Some consequences of individual differences in the acquisition of literacy. *Reading Research Quarterly, 21,* 360–407.

Stanovich, K. E., & Siegel, L. S. (1994). Phenotypic performance profile of children with reading disabilities: A regression-based test of phonological-core difference model. *Journal of Educational Psychology, 86,* 24–53.

Stanovich, K. E., Cunningham, A. E., & Freeman, J. (1984). Intelligence, cognitive skills, and early reading progress. *Reading Research Quarterly, 14,* 278–303.

Stahl, S. A., & Murray, B. A. (1994). Phonological awareness and its relationship to early reading. *Journal of Educational Psychology, 86,* 221–234.

Sulzby, E. (1985). Children's emergent reading of favorite storybooks: A developmental study. *Reading Research Quarterly, 20,* 458–481.

Swanson, H. L. (1992). Generality and modifiability of working memory among skilled and less skilled readers. *Journal of Educational Psychology, 84,* 473–488.

Tangel, D., & Blachman, B. (1992). Effect of phonemic awareness instruction on kindergarten children's invented spelling. *Journal of Reading Behavior, 24,* 233–261.

Thomas, K. (1985). Early reading as a social interaction process. *Language Arts, 62,* 469–475.

Torgesen, J. K. (1988). Studies of children with learning disabilities who perform poorly on memory span tasks. *Journal of Learning Disabilities, 21,* 605–615.

Torgesen, J. K., & Mathes, P. (2000). *A Basic Guide to Understanding, Assessing, and Teaching Phonological Awareness.* Austin, TX: PRO-ED.

Torgesen, J. K., Rashotte, C., Alexander, A. W., Alexander, J., & MacPhee, K. (2003). Progress towards understanding the instructional conditions necessary for remediating reading difficulties in older children. In B. Foorman (Ed.), *Preventing and Remediating Reading Difficulties: Bringing Science to Scale* (pp. 275–298). Baltimore: York Press.

Treiman, R., & Tincoff, R. (1997). The fragility of alphabetic principle. Children's knowledge of letter names can cause them to spell syllabically rather than alphabetically. *Journal of Experimental Child Psychology, 64,* 425–451.

Vandervelden, M. C., & Siegel, L. S. (1997). Teaching phonological processing skills in early literacy: A developmental approach. *Learning Disabilities Quarterly, 20,* 63–81.

Vellutino, F. R., Scanlon, D. M., & Lyon, G. R. (2000). Differentiating between difficult to remediate and readily remediated poor readers: More evidence against the IQ-achievement discrepancy definition of reading disability. *Journal of Learning Disabilities, 33,* 223–238.

Vellutino, F. R., Scanlon, D. M., Sipay, E. R., Small, S. G., Pratt, A., Chen, R., et al. (1996). Cognitive profiles of difficult to remediate and readily remediated poor readers: Early intervention as a vehicle for distinguishing between cognitive and experiential deficits as basic causes of specific reading disability. *Journal of Educational Psychology, 88,* 601–638.

Wagner, R., Torgesen, J. K., Laughon, P., Simmons, K., & Rashotte, C. A. (1993). Development of young readers' phonological processing abilities. *Journal of Educational Psychology, 85,* 83–103.

Wolf, M., & Bowers, P. G. (1999). The double deficit hypothesis for the development of dyslexia. *Journal of Educational Psychology, 91,* 415–438.

Worden, P. E., & Boettcher, W. (1990). Young children's acquisition of alphabet knowledge. *Journal of Reading Behavior, 22,* 277–295.

Zutell, J. (1998). Word sorting: A developmental spelling approach to word study for delayed readers. *Reading and Writing Quarterly, 14,* 219–238.

Chapter 2

Environmental Factors and Other Characteristics of Children Who Face Challenges in Becoming Literate

Ecological factors are those that are a result of the interaction between an organism and its environment. B. F. Skinner said that when humans interact with their environment, the outcome is behavior. For some of us, learning to read occurred rather smoothly during the round robin reading group lessons that were prevalent during the 1970s. For some children, this method was not sufficient for teaching reading, even though they were placed in a group where books were on their same reading level. This method could have been insufficient for various reasons. One explanation might be the lack of opportunities to engage in storybook reading before entering formal schooling. Another explanation may be the lack of opportunities to read in the round-robin group format or lack of direct instruction on reading skills before children read in their groups. Finally, difficulty learning to read might be due to the combination of limited experiences before and during formal schooling.

Often the reasons for children's difficulties in learning to read or their not reading at proficient levels are not as important as efforts to target and implement appropriate types of instruction to help children learn to read or progress toward becoming proficient readers. However, research that sought to uncover explanations for a failure to thrive in the world of literature and its many genres has provided avenues for implementing prevention services.

School psychologists need to be aware of the possible reasons why children face challenges to becoming literate so that, as professionals, they are in a better position to advocate for prevention and intervention services. Establishing home-school collaborative partnerships is paramount to meeting the literacy needs of children. Collaboration begins with recognizing that parental involvement is an extremely important contributing factor in children's literacy development.

PARENTAL INVOLVEMENT

Parents' beliefs about their role in their child's literacy development may be important to ascertain during conferences with the parents. Studies have shown that children interacted with books more often and experienced high-quality interactions with books, such as joint storybook reading with their parents, if their parents believed in playing a significant role in fostering their child's development in literacy skills, believed in reading as an important skill to gain information, and believed in facilitating active participation from their child such as reading aloud (DeBaryshe, 1995; Shonnenschein, Baker, Serpell, & Schmidt, 2000). Though to a certain degree beliefs may be predictive of actual occurrences of parents' involvement in their child's literacy development, it is important to gather information through direct observations of the actual interactions related to literacy growth between parents and their child.

Parental involvement begins before children enter formal schooling. According to Burgess, Hecht, and Lonigan (2002), home literacy environments can be conceptualized as limiting, passive, or active. A *limiting* home literacy environment is classified as limiting based on parents' education level and school experiences, household income, and parents' reading level. Children who resided in limiting home literacy environments had lower levels of oral language skills, phonological skills, letter-sound correspondences, and word reading skills (Burgess et al., 2002). Research has revealed that parents' education levels significantly correlated with children's language development and reading achievement (Christian, Morrison, & Bryant, 1998). A *passive* home literacy environment is one in which children observe and inquire about their parents' engagement in literacy activities such as reading for enjoyment and writing regularly. These parents are likely to have large vocabularies and thus interact with each other and their children using a large vocabulary. Positive reading outcomes were observed in children who resided in homes where parents spent considerable time reading and gained personal enjoyment from reading (Shonnenschein, Brody, & Munsterman, 1996).

An *active* home literacy environment consists of parents who directly engage their children in literacy activities. Active parent participation with regard to early literacy experiences provided to children in the home strongly predicted children's early language and literacy development (Roberts, Jurgens, & Burchinal, 2005). An example of an active environmental literacy activity would be joint storybook reading between a parent and a child, especially if dyadic verbal interactions occur throughout the reading of the story (Edwards, 1995). Through a meta-analysis of studies involving early literacy development, Bus, van Ijzendoorn, and Pellegrini (1995) found that joint storybook reading was positively related to literacy outcomes for preschool children. Higher language outcomes were achieved when a group of preschool children and their parents engaged in joint storybook reading, as opposed to a group of preschool children who engaged in joint storybook reading in a reading group with their peers (Lonigan & Whitehurst, 1998). In addition to joint storybook reading, other literacy-related activities that occurred between parents and their child, such as singing songs, producing rhymes, and telling stories, contributed to positive literacy outcomes for young children (Bennett, Weigel, & Martin, 2002).

It is important to note that not all low-income families have a limiting home literacy environment. Some low-income families take advantage of the services provided in their local community by taking frequent trips to the library, learning about charity donation services, and purchasing bargain books at local garage sales, Goodwill stores, or bookstores. Additionally, many low-income families enroll their children in early intervention programs such as Head Start. Such programs are certainly needed for children who may not have access to vast amounts of literacy materials at home and limited opportunities to engage in early literacy activities, but these programs do not take the place of rich literacy home environments. In a study conducted on children who attended a Head Start program, Bryant, Burchinal, Lau, and Sparling (1994) found that children benefited more from the program if they resided in enriching home environments than children who experienced very little opportunity to interact with literature or literacy-related activities.

HOME-SCHOOL COLLABORATION

Children's development in literacy skills is strengthened when home and school literacy activities and practices are well coordinated and support each other (McNaughton, 1995; Waldbart, Meyers, & Meyers, 2006), making this connection between home and school a critical ecological factor in the development of literacy. Investigations have attested to more positive literacy-related outcomes for children who received well-coordinated literacy practices between home and school, in contrast to children who received literacy practices in either the home or school alone (Morrow & Young, 1997; Lonigan & Whitehurst, 1998). Although research has demonstrated the powerful effects of consistency between teacher literacy habits and parental literacy habits, this connection may not be occurring for some children who are referred to school psychologists and other educational consultants for literacy problems. To achieve well-coordinated practices between home and school, family-school collaboration models should be applied. Additionally, collaborative efforts are likely to result in the consideration of culturally specific practices that may be different from or inconsistent with the practices at school (Nastasi, Moore, & Varjas, 2004).

Conjoint Family-School Collaboration Model

A model that has demonstrated sound scientific support is called the conjoint family-school collaboration model, which was developed and evaluated by Sheridan and her colleagues (e.g., Sheridan & Kratochwill, 1992; Sheridan, Kratochwill, & Bergan, 1996; Welch & Sheridan, 1995). The term *conjoint* is a powerful word for describing this model because it involves the joint forces of educators and families helping children to develop academically, socially, vocationally, and emotionally through positive healthy actions (Conoley & Sheridan, 2005).

A common goal must be established between home and school at the start of a collaborative relationship. The goal should focus on positive outcomes for the child. Once this goal is established, which places the child as the central focus, family and school personnel jointly undergo several phases, including (1) needs identification, (2) needs analysis and intervention development, (3) plan intervention implementation, (4) plan evaluation, and (5) analysis. In the needs identification phase, shared concerns about the child's literacy development are identified and prioritized so that one or two specific literacy needs are addressed initially (Sheridan, Kratochwill, & Bergan, 1996). Once one or two specific needs are identified, a discussion will address how data will be collected to determine the severity of the literacy need. Data generated from assessments are important to gather to determine what skills the students have mastered and what skills need to be developed further. Assessments should also address the child's functioning within the context of the conditions under which the child is expected to learn and achieve. A number of assessment tools are available to assess various aspects of literacy development (these assessments will be discussed in detail in the next section of this book).

Once data have been obtained, the team of professionals and family members meet to discuss and analyze the data to determine literacy functioning levels and the conditions that may be influencing literacy performance levels (needs analysis). In conjunction with this needs analysis, an intervention plan is developed collaboratively by family members and educators. The plan consists of literacy activities and procedures for implementing those activities that can be easily carried out in both home and school environments. The implementation plan also consists of family members' and school members' participation in implementing the plan. Parents were actually found to prefer to participate in meaningful ways, such as implementing teaching strategies or techniques when assisting their child's learning (Christenson, Hurly, Sheridan, & Fenstermacher, 1997). For example, parents asked if a researcher would be interested in sharing the phonic technique that was used in an investigation to teach children word-decoding skills so the parents could continue to use it at home at the completion of the study (Joseph, 1998/1999).

In the plan implementation phase, family members and educators play a role and share the responsibility. The professionals may need to model or demonstrate how to implement certain literacy activities so that all parties know how to perform the activities. This, in part, ensures the likelihood that activities are performed as planned. For instance, some parents do not know how to engage in joint storybook reading with their children. An educator may need to visit the home to model or demonstrate how to share the reading of a story with a child and how to ask questions that guide children to think about the contents in the reading and allow children to ask questions about what they are reading. In other words, demonstrating dialogic reading may be necessary if family members do not have such interactions in their natural repertoire of communication. In general, home visits have resulted in an increase in parent-child literacy interactions (Nistler & Maiers, 1999).

While the intervention plan is being implemented, literacy behaviors and performance should be tracked through progress-monitoring assessments or data gathering procedures to determine if the intervention is resulting in the desired literacy outcomes (the goals determined by the collaborative team members). The evaluation that follows monitoring involves analyzing and discussing the data that were gathered throughout the process (prior to and during the implementation of the intervention). Team members can determine whether and how responsive the child was to the intervention plan that was implemented at home and at school. At this time, the intervention plan may need to be modified. If the intervention met the desired literacy goals and needs of the child, then the process begins again with problem identification to target other literacy skills that need to be addressed.

Figure 2-1 illustrates a case example of the use of conjoint collaboration with a child referred for literacy skill needs. In this example, Jennifer was referred for needs in the area of reading, and the team of professionals determined that she needed to increase fluency levels in oral reading. In this example, the responsibility was shared between home and school team members as the same intervention—repeated readings, a simple, cost-effective and time-efficient procedure—was applied across settings and monitored using the same recording technique. Applying the same intervention across home and school settings increases the opportunities for building fluency in multiple contexts. In this case, it helps Jennifer realize that more than one party on her team values her becoming a fluent reader, and she recognizes that support between parties exists to help her achieve her goals in both home and school contexts.

Using a well-established model and systematically applying its phases are the science of successful partnerships. However, the "art" of successful partnerships—the mutual respect and healthy positive interactions between parents and professionals (that is, communication)—is an important key to the success of their collaboration (Esler, Godber, & Christenson, 2002). Ways to achieve communication and build trust include sharing some positive observations with parents about their child's reading skills, allowing parents to voice their opinions and concerns, listening to parents' concerns and the ways they have assisted in the past, keeping the focus of the conversation on helping the child be a more successful reader, providing information that may help parents promote literacy skills in their child, and sharing the responsibility for helping their child develop literacy skills (Christenson & Hirsch, 1998).

Identification of Homes in Need of Rich Literacy Experiences

Before many children enter formal schooling in the United States, they have been exposed to print and have had print-related experiences in various contexts, developed concepts about print, have knowledge of narratives and discourse patterns, and discovered the entertainment value of reading by observing and interacting with their parents on literacy-related activities (Snow & Tabors, 1996). Just as there are many children who enter formal schooling with rich literacy experiences in their developmental history, there are some who enter the world of literacy at the same time that they enter their formal schooling years (Snow, Burns, & Griffin, 1998).

Figure 2-1. *Conjoint collaboration case study of Jennifer.*

Needs identification: Through an interview format, parents and educators defined Jennifer's needs as poor reading passage fluency skills.

Needs analysis: Curriculum-based reading passage rate measures were administered to determine the severity of Jennifer's poor oral reading passage fluency skills. Three passages were administered and the number of words read correctly per minute was recorded and averaged across three passages. Jennifer read 98 percent of the words correctly in the passages, but she only read an average of thirty words per minute.

Plan: Parents and educators decided to increase Jennifer's fluency levels by having her engage in repeated readings of passages at least three times at home and school. During every reading of the passage, she would be timed for one minute, and the number of words read correctly per minute would be recorded on a chart by Jennifer and a peer, teacher, sibling, or parent.

Implementation of the plan: Mom, Dad, and older sister took turns having Jennifer orally read a story, then reread the story two times for a minute every evening for three weeks. Words read correctly per minute during each reading of the passage were recorded on a chart by Jennifer and either Mom, Dad, or older sister. At school, the teacher's assistant had Jennifer complete the same repeated reading exercise, and her performance was recorded every day over a three-week period.

Plan evaluation: Parents and educators met at the end of the first week to evaluate how well the plan was being carried out and if there were any questions regarding the plan. The team met again at the end of three weeks to evaluate the data recorded on the charts. It was determined that Jennifer made considerable progress in the number of words read per minute. Parents and educators noted that Jennifer read with more expression as her fluency levels increased but that there was room for improvement, so they decided to incorporate listening while reading so Jennifer could listen to a proficient reader read a story with expression before reading it herself.

There is not a more opportune time to involve parents in meaningful ways in their children's literacy development than when their children are very young and are beginning some type of schooling. Parents, just like their very young children, are eager to learn and are excited about all the academic (preacademic) possibilities at school.

Despite the fact that most, if not all, parents are excited and eager to help their very young children be successful in their early academic development, they may not necessarily know how to identify resources that would help them support their children's growth. For instance, some families who live in poverty may want their children to have an awareness of print, but they may have very few objects around the house (especially those with print on them), including very few pictures on the walls or decorative objects on the furniture, no shopping lists hung on the refrigerator, no technology with appropriate print literature or word processing programs, no newspapers or magazines, limited household or cleaning supplies with printed labels on them, and no books.

School psychologists and other educational consultants can play a significant role in working with preschool, day care, and Head Start coordinators or directors as well as teachers to identify families who are in need of enriched literacy experiences at home. A team of professionals who works in the schools, such as school psychologists, speech and language therapists, reading specialists, early childhood specialists, and teachers, can work together to create resource materials that support early literacy experiences at school and can be made readily available to families for use at home. The team should also plan who will model the use of these techniques or materials, if necessary, such as identifying all the things in the house that begin with the sound /a/, or doing storytelling with picture books. Additionally, a mechanism for following up to support the continued use of these techniques and materials should be established.

Collaboration Between Home, School, and Child-Care Facilities

Likewise, early childhood specialists can play a unique role in facilitating literacy growth between community agencies and families, especially given the likely fact that both parents are employed outside of the home or a single parent is employed full time. Many young children spend a considerable part of their day in a child-care facility or privately operated home child-care setup. Child-care workers can be a part of the team to model, design, and implement rich literacy activities for children. Weigel, Martin, and Bennett (2005) found that preschool children who attended a child-care facility benefited the most in their development of early literacy skills when child-care facilities provided literacy-related activities that were consistent with those provided at home. The key finding of this study implied that if preschool children attended a child-care facility, they were more likely to grow stronger in their early literacy skills if literacy habits were practiced at home and at the child-care facility rather than only in one setting and not the other. This investigation provided further evidence that consistency between environments where children spend considerable amounts of time is critical to enhancing children's success.

CHARACTERISTICS OF READERS

Expert Readers

Expert readers are fluent readers, meaning that they read multiple types of texts accurately, quickly, and with expression. They apply word identification skills successfully without assistance when they encounter words that are unfamiliar to them. They primarily read text to gain meaning. They know how to read for multiple purposes (e.g., reading directions for putting equipment together, reading a mystery novel for enjoyment, reading science textbooks to learn about biological concepts for an upcoming exam). Expert readers have multiple strategies for gaining meaning from print, and they monitor their reading and check for understanding of content (Pressley, 1999).

Novice Readers

All children with reading problems, despite their categorical label, can be considered novice readers because they are not yet proficient. Essentially, novice readers do not perform literacy skills effortlessly as expert readers do. Approximately 80 percent of children identified with learning disabilities have difficulties in reading (Lerner, 1997). Even though the majority of children identified with learning disabilities have reading problems, those problems are not likely to be diagnosed until the age of nine (Shaywitz, 1998). Children with severe reading problems are often characterized in various ways (e.g., dyslexic, learning disabled, developmentally delayed). However, despite their label, many children with reading problems need to learn similar basic skills, depending on the type and severity of their reading problems.

Circular language or reasoning is often used when diagnostic labels are applied to children to explain why they have difficulty learning to read. In other words, labels are often used to explain other labels. For instance, educators often say that a child has a learning disability because he or she has a reading disability or is dyslexic. These explanations have very little meaning in terms of describing the nature of the child's difficulties, making it difficult to target appropriate types of instruction. However, a brief discussion about various diagnostic labels associated with children with reading problems is provided. These labels are often used in reference to children with reading problems, even though their meaning as used may vary. Children with basic reading problems are generally classified in one of two or three categories of reading disabilities: delayed readers, garden-variety types, and dyslexia. From a description of these categories, some may readily decipher that the definitions and characteristics that describe these types of reading disabilities overlap.

Delayed Readers and Garden-Variety Types

A delayed reader is anyone who is not performing up to his or her potential or ability in reading (McCormick, 2003). These individuals can progress through the acquisition phases of reading but may do so at slower rates. Children who are characterized as having garden-variety types of reading difficulties are those who perform below average on reading achievement measures and also have below-average intelligence (not in the mental retardation range); below-average spoken, receptive, and written language; and below-average performance across other academic content areas such as arithmetic, social studies, and science (Stanovich, 1988). These children are often labeled "at risk" for academic failure, but they are not eligible for special education services because no significant discrepancy exists between their intellectual ability and their reading achievement (if that measure is used by professionals in their school districts).

Dyslexia

Children who are classified as dyslexic have reading problems that are associated with neurological dysfunctions. Children who are said to have dyslexia make up the smaller percentage of children with reading problems (Shaywitz, Escobar, Shaywitz, & Fletcher, 1992). A substitute term for dyslexia is *severe reading disability* (McCormick, 2003). These children's reading difficulties are those that cannot be explained by a lack of instruction or poor instruction, mental retardation, or limited literacy environmental conditions. These children have average or above-average intellectual abilities and receptive language skills. A genetic link is often associated with children with very severe reading disabilities or those classified as dyslexic (Grigorenko, 2001). This means that chances are a biological family member (parent, aunt, uncle, cousin, etc.) also had very severe reading disabilities or dyslexia. Children with severe reading disabilities or dyslexia may perform satisfactorily in other academic content areas such as mathematics as long as the demand for literacy skills is minimal, making this disability domain specific to skills associated with word recognition or word reading (Stanovich, 1991). Slow working memory, particularly slow phonological memory (Breznitz, 1997), slow word retrieval resulting in speech production difficulties (Breznitz, 1997), rapid automatized naming (Wolf & Bowers, 1999), phonemic awareness difficulties (Stanovich, 1992), orthographic skill difficulties (Stanovich, 1992) and linking of phonological with orthographic information difficulties (Breznitz, 2002) are among the literacy factors associated with developmental dyslexia. According to Breznitz and Berman (2003), an underlying cause of dyslexia may be a physiologically based reduction in the speed of processing the connection between phonological and orthographic information. This may be the reason why children identified with very severe reading difficulties or dyslexia exhibit slow rates in making print-to-sound conversions despite instructional opportunities.

Snowling (2000) described two subtypes of children with dyslexia. One subtype is referred to as *phonologic dyslexics*; the other type is referred to as *surface dyslexics*. Phonologic dyslexics have extreme difficulty decoding words, including pseudowords (e.g., *nat, lut*), but they may be able to decode some words with irregular spellings (e.g., *what, sleigh*). Surface dyslexics can decode words with regular spelling patterns better than they can decode words with irregular spelling patterns.

When professionals and parents observe directionality problems in reading, or scattered or staircase eye movements during reading, they often associate those problems with dyslexia. Parents often ask school psychologists if they think their child is dyslexic when their child reads letters, words, or phrases backward or when their child claims that the "words are jumping off the page." These types of reading behaviors are often considered to be symptoms rather than causes of reading difficulties (Pressley, 1999). Children who have limited word identification and recognition (word reading) skills may exhibit directionality problems from not learning to read from a left to right and top to bottom orientation.

If they are unable to read the majority of words on a page, their eyes naturally skip to those words that they can read or attempt to identify. This skipping across and down the page results in habitual staircase (zigzag) reading (imposed eye movements rather than a left to right and back to left sweeping movement at the end of each line). Eye training exercises provided by vision specialists have not been proven to be effective, because the underlying problem is word reading skills rather than eye movement abnormalities (Rayner, 1992). Good readers actually read every word in every line of meaningful text, despite speculation that "good readers skim text." This has been proven by researchers using computer-mediated eye monitoring technology, who examined eye movements and eye fixations on words (see Rayner & Pollatsek, 1989, for a review).

Mental Retardation

Children with mental retardation are individuals who have an IQ that is classified as subaverage intellectual functioning (70 or below). These individuals may actually be reading in accordance with their cognitive ability levels or potential. However, they are often observed to read at much slower rates than the average and above-average IQ peers (90 and above; McCormick, 2003). If children are not achieving at their potential, this could mean that they are not receiving appropriate instruction. It is important for school psychologists and educators to realize that children with mental retardation can be taught how to read and can progress substantially in their literacy development. Children with mental retardation will likely need systematic instructional reading procedures and more exposure and opportunities to practice reading words and other reading skills than their typically developing peers (Love & Litton, 1994).

Children with mental retardation are an underrepresented research group among children with reading problems. For instance, only a handful of studies in the past decade have investigated the effects of phonics instruction on children with mental retardation (see Joseph & Seery, 2004, for a review). Most studies have focused on examining the effectiveness of teaching sight (whole) word reading skills to children with mental retardation, even those children who function at very low cognitive ability levels (see Browder & Xin, 1998, for a review). Katims (2000) noted that little attention is given to reading instruction for children with mild to moderate mental retardation in higher educational institutions and in textbooks used to train special educators. Children with extremely low cognitive ability levels (IQ 50 and below), along with communication and other complications, can be taught functional reading skills. For instance, they learn to read signs and labels of food products and other products at the grocery store, along with some basic sight words, so that they can perform daily living activities.

Nonlabel Characteristics

Although etiology may be important for gaining an understanding about children, it tells professionals little about the specific skills that need to be developed. Instead, many professionals and parents often become lost or mystified by the label, leading them to "admire" the problem or become hindered by the label, rather than move forward to problem-solving, solution-focused, or positive actions that have a probability of helping children. Children with difficulties in the area of reading may be either "won't do" or "can't do" learners (Witt & Beck, 1999). *Won't do* children are those that can read but choose not to for various reasons. These children may need interventions, such as positive reinforcement, that are targeted at encouraging engaged behavior. *Can't do* children are those that primarily need explicit (direct) skill instruction.

There are many areas of skill difficulties that characterize children as needing specialized services. These skill difficulties were discussed in chapter 1 and are revisited in the context of assessment and interventions in subsequent chapters. These skill difficulties may consist of phonemic awareness skills, word identification, whole word or sight word recognition, oral reading skills, fluent reading (reading quickly, accurately, and with expression), reading vocabulary, reading comprehension, and reading comprehension rate. Within these broader skill areas are specific subskills, such as identifying words with consonant blends and making inferences while reading text. It is important for school psychologists and other professionals to focus on identifying specific skill needs within broader skill domains so that observable and measurable goals and objectives can be generated. Identifying the student's specific needs allows professionals to target an intervention to those needs, thereby increasing the likelihood that the student will respond positively to the intervention and make observable progress in acquiring literacy skills.

Special Considerations for Culturally and Linguistically Diverse Students

School psychologists and other educational professionals are increasingly consulted about how to best work with individuals from culturally and linguistically diverse families. A growing number of individuals living in the United States are from culturally and linguistically diverse backgrounds. Immigration to the United States has increased significantly in the past decade (U.S. Immigration and Naturalization Service, 2002). The term *diverse* is a very broad one, encompassing not only individuals who are identified with disabilities but also those who are culturally and linguistically different from the mainstream. Culturally diverse students come from a multitude of socioeconomic backgrounds and linguistic skills. Some may speak standard English fluently whereas others speak nonstandard English or are bilingual, or do not speak standard English at all (McCormick, 2003). If these individuals have difficulty with reading in their native language, it is likely they will also experience difficulty reading in their new language. These individuals often have similar types of difficulties that culturally mainstream children experience. However, some special factors need to be considered by those who work with individuals from culturally and linguistically diverse backgrounds.

Cultural considerations related to children's reading development include vocabulary and use of concepts. Children from other cultures may use terms or concepts that are not typically used in mainstream North American culture, depending on what part of the country they live. The value systems may vary from culture to culture. For some, working and developing reading skills independently may not be as valued as working and developing reading skills in a group. Schedules of reinforcement for accomplishments in developing literacy skills may be valued differently from one culture to the next. For instance, delayed reinforcement or gratification is valued in middle-class American culture, but immediate reinforcement is expected in other cultures. Generally, mainstream Americans work by the clock and value adhering to time constraints when completing assignments, whereas time may not be a critical variable for other cultural groups.

Linguistic considerations include dialects that are not standard North American. Though regional dialects are viewed favorably, such as "Deep South" dialects versus "Northeastern" dialects, grammatically different dialects, both syntax and semantics, may be perceived negatively. Languages different from standard English may not be structured the same way phonologically, syntactically, and semantically. A student's pronunciation of certain sounds may be different, but those differences may not necessarily change the meaning of the concept for that student.

With regard to helping children develop reading skills in standard English, learning about cultural and linguistic differences is important so that these factors can be taken into consideration, and so children are not misidentified or labeled. According to the National Research Council (2002), individuals from culturally diverse groups are over-represented in disability categories such as learning disabilities, mental retardation, attention deficit, and emotional disturbance. Most importantly, the focus should remain on helping children learn reading skills and succeed in reading standard English literature if this is the common practice that will allow them to pursue a multitude of employment opportunities and increase their quality of life in the United States. Professionals need to be careful that they do not accept differences in ways that interfere with children's learning of essential skills such as reading (McCormick, 2003). Teachers should execute effective teaching principles (e.g., those described in chapter 4 of this book), including for instance providing students with ample opportunities to practice reading their list of basic sight words despite linguistic differences; otherwise the students may not be able to participate in reading stories along with the other children in class. In other words, although educators should be understanding of students' linguistic differences and should not be punitive if reading skills do not develop as quickly as mainstream students, educators should not relinquish the many opportunities that should be provided to children with linguistic differences. Some studies suggest that intensive small-group reading instruction is effective for helping English language learners improve their reading performance (e.g., Gerber et al., 2004; Graves, Gersten, & Haager, 2004; Haager & Windmueller, 2001; Vaughn, Linan-Thompson, & Hickman, 2003).

Neuman (1999) and Klinger and Edwards (2006) advocate a culturally responsive approach to providing instruction to all children. Being culturally responsive means understanding that all children learn in sociocultural contexts. Features of this approach include respecting and appreciating children's home cultures and realizing that being culturally diverse is not synonymous with lacking rich literature or high-quality literacy experiences at home. Students need healthy collaborative interactions with adults as well as with peers in the school community. The same standards of reading achievement are expected and applied for children of diverse cultures as for mainstream children in the classroom. However, effective educators realize that to help children of diverse cultures achieve those standards, they need to use instructional approaches that address individual needs and include multicultural literature resources. For instance, they can provide appropriate strategies and literacy resources to parents so that they are empowered to help their child succeed (e.g., storybooks that reflect each family's culture). Finally, Neuman (1999) emphasizes establishing continuity and collaboration between home and school so that children are not receiving conflicting messages while simultaneously building on their cultural and linguistic backgrounds.

Older Delayed Readers

As mentioned earlier, instruction and opportunities to engage children in rich literacy experiences should begin before they enter kindergarten. The type of literacy instruction in kindergarten and first grade has long-lasting effects on children's reading achievement as they progress to subsequent grades (Alexander & Entwisle, 1996; Torgesen, 2000). Children who experienced good instruction in the first grade performed better on reading achievement tests in subsequent grades than children who had poor instruction in first grade, despite better instruction in subsequent grades, making the early years in school very critical in relation to long-term student success (Pianta, 1990). However, although instruction is critical in the primary grades, it is never too late to learn how to read. Effective literacy instruction should also be an important focus for secondary schools. Older delayed readers have been characterized as failure-avoidance or failure-accepting students, meaning that they either avoid challenging academic tasks and only attempt easy ones, or they do not attempt any type of tasks and fail to complete all assignments, which often leads to dropping out of school.

The International Reading Association developed a position statement for teaching adolescents reading skills. The position statement reflected children's need for instruction that builds fundamental literacy skills and their desire to read increasingly higher-level texts (Moore, Bean, Birdyshaw, & Rycik, 1999, p. 102). Many adolescents who cannot read fluently still want to achieve this goal even though they may not vocalize this to their peers. Reading is essential to using technology, accessing information, obtaining and holding a job, and performing activities that enhance the quality of life.

Even older students must be able to read material at a basic level first so they have a repertoire of words they can automatically read and on which they can build new vocabulary when they eventually advance to higher-level texts with abstract conceptual relationships (Salinger, 2003). Most reading material is written at a fourth-grade level, which is achievable for high school students who have limited reading skills. Instruction at all grade levels and ages of children should be responsive to children's needs so that real learning has a chance to take place (Daly, Chafouleas, & Skinner, 2005). Quality and quantity of instruction should be considered when examining its effectiveness at meeting children's literacy needs.

WHAT CAN SCHOOL PSYCHOLOGISTS AND OTHER EDUCATIONAL CONSULTANTS DO?

1. Refrain from making assumptions about individuals despite socioeconomic status or other stereotypical characteristics regarding the extent to which parents wish to be involved in their children's literacy development.
2. Work with preschool, kindergarten, and primary grade coordinators/directors and teachers to identify families who need help establishing literacy-rich home environments for their children, and then have the team of professionals collaborate with families to establish rich literacy experiences at school and at home.
3. Involve parents in meaningful ways in helping children develop their literacy skills.
4. Share the responsibility of educating children on literacy skills and establish consistency between teacher and parent literacy habits and continuity between school and home.
5. Communicate with parents frequently and openly using inclusive language when discussing how their children are progressing on literacy skills at school.
6. Model or demonstrate to parents how to implement evidence-based instruction techniques, lessons, or programs designed to foster literacy skills.
7. Develop progress-monitoring methods for parents to use at home and demonstrate how to implement and evaluate them.
8. Help parents gather literature materials (e.g., books, magazines, and phonics programs).
9. Refrain from using language that is circular (e.g., "your child has a learning disability because he has reading problems"). Instead, define reading difficulties in terms of specific skills (observable and measurable) that need to be learned.
10. Recognize the powerful impact of instruction at both the primary and secondary levels.
11. Encourage optimism about children's and adolescents' potential for learning despite the severity of their difficulties.
12. Strongly respect and embrace children's cultural and linguistic origins.
13. Help educators remain focused on helping children achieve the literacy goals of learning to read and becoming proficient readers despite their less than optimal home environments.

SUMMARY POINTS

- Parental beliefs play a significant role in children's literacy development.
- Home literacy environments can be conceptualized as limiting, passive, or active.
- Early childhood consultants can help coordinate literacy activities between school, community agencies, and home.

- Children can be characterized as novice or expert readers.
- Stating that a student has a learning disability because he or she is dyslexic is considered to be circular reasoning; it does not explain the child's reading difficulties.
- Consultants may consider using a culturally responsive approach and realize that being culturally diverse is not synonymous with lacking high-quality literacy experiences at home.
- Older delayed readers need instruction that builds on basic literacy skills.

QUESTIONS FOR DISCUSSION

1. What is conjoint school-family collaboration?
2. Why might conjoint collaboration be especially beneficial for a child residing in a limiting home literacy environment?
3. What are the similarities among students who are characterized as delayed readers, children with garden-variety types of reading difficulties, and children with dyslexia?
4. How might an educator address a "won't do" problem versus a "can't do" problem?
5. Why is it important for educators to take cultural and linguistic differences into account when considering reading performance?

REFERENCES

Alexander, K., & Entwisle, D. R. (1996). Schools and children at risk. In A. Booth & J. Dunn (Eds.), *Family and School Links: How Do They Affect Educational Outcomes?* (pp. 67–88). Hillsdale, NJ: Erlbaum.

Bennett, K. K., Weigel, D. J., & Martin, S. S. (2002). Children's acquisition of early literacy skills: Examining family contributions. *Early Childhood Research Quarterly, 17*, 295–317.

Breznitz, Z. (1997). The effect of accelerated reading on memory for text among dyslexic readers. *Journal of Educational Psychology, 89*, 287–299.

Breznitz, Z. (2002). Asynchrony of visual-orthographic and auditory-phonological word recognition processes: An underlying factor in dyslexia. *Reading and Writing: An International Quarterly, 15*, 15–42.

Breznitz, Z., & Berman, L. (2003). The underlying factors in word reading rate. *Educational Psychology Review, 15*, 247–265.

Browder, D., & Xin, Y. P. (1998). A meta-analysis and review of sight word research and its implications for teaching functional reading to individuals with moderate to severe disabilities. *Journal of Special Education, 32*, 130–153.

Bryant, P. E., Burchinal, M., Lau, L. B., & Sparling, J. J. (1994). Family and classroom correlates of Head Start children's developmental outcomes. *Early Childhood Research Quarterly*, 9, 289–310.

Burgess, S. R., Hecht, S. A., & Lonigan, C. J. (2002). Relations of the home literacy environment (HLE) to the development of reading-related abilities: A one year longitudinal study. *Reading Research Quarterly*, 37, 408–426.

Bus, A. G., van Ijzendoorn, M. H., & Pellegrini, A. D. (1995). Joint storybook reading makes for success in learning to read: A meta-analysis on intergenerational transmission of literacy. *Review of Educational Research*, 65, 1–21.

Christenson, S. L., & Hirsch, J. (1998). Facilating partnerships and conflict resolution between families and schools. In K. C. Stoiber & T. R. Kratochwill (Eds.), *Handbook of group intervention for children and families* (pp. 307–344). Boston: Allyn & Bacon.

Christenson, S. L., Hurly, C. M., Sheridan, S. M., & Fenstermacher, K. (1997). Parents' and school psychologists' perspectives on parent involvement activities. *School Psychology Review*, 26, 111–130.

Christian, K., Morrison, F. J., & Bryant, F. B. (1998). Predicting kindergarten academic skills. Interactions among child care, maternal education, and family literacy environments. *Early Childhood Research Quarterly*, 13, 501–521.

Conoley, J. C., & Sheridan, S. M. (2005). Understanding and implementing school-family interventions after neuropsychological impairment. In R. C. D'Amato, E. Fletcher-Janzen, & C. Reynolds (Eds.), *Handbook of School Neuropsychology*. Hoboken, NJ: John Wiley & Sons.

Daly, E. J., III, Chafouleas, S., & Skinner, C. H. (2005). *Interventions for Reading Problems: Designing and Evaluating Effective Strategies*. New York: Guilford Press.

DeBaryshe, D. B. (1995). Maternal belief systems: Linchpin in the home reading process. *Journal of Applied Developmental Psychology*, 16, 1–20.

Edwards, P. A. (1995). Empowering low-income mothers and fathers to share books with young children. *The Reading Teacher*, 48, 558–564.

Esler, A. N., Godber, Y., & Christenson, S. L. (2002). Best practices in supporting home-school collaboration. In A. Thomas & J. Grimes (Eds.), *Best Practices in School Psychology IV* (pp. 389–411). Bethesda, MD: National Association of School Psychologists.

Gerber, M. M., Jimenez, T., Leafstedt, J., Villaruz, J., Richards, C., & English, J. (2004). English reading effects of small-group intensive intervention in Spanish for English learners. *Learning Disabilities Research & Practice, 19,* 239–251.

Graves, A., Gersten, R., & Haager, D. (2004). Literacy instruction in multiple-language first-grade classrooms. Linking student outcomes to observed instructional practice. *Learning Disabilities Research & Practice, 19,* 262–272.

Grigorenko, E. L. (2001). Developmental dyslexia: An update on genes, brains, and environments. *Journal of Child Psychology and Psychiatry, 42,* 91–125.

Haager, D., & Windmueller, M. P. (2001). Early reading intervention for English language learners at-risk for learning disabilities: Student and teacher outcomes in an urban school. *Learning Disability Quarterly, 24,* 235–250.

Joseph, L. M. (1998/1999). Word boxes help children with learning disabilities identify and spell words. *The Reading Teacher, 42,* 348–356.

Joseph, L. M., & Seery, M. E. (2004). Where is the phonics? An updated review on the use of phonics with students with mental retardation. *Remedial and Special Education, 25,* 88–94.

Katims, D. S. (2000). Literacy instruction for people with mental retardation. Historical highlights and contemporary analysis. *Education and Training in Mental Retardation and Developmental Disabilities, 35,* 3–15.

Klinger, J. K., & Edwards, P. A. (2006). Cultural considerations with response to intervention models. *Reading Research Quarterly, 41,* 108–117.

Lerner, J. (1997). *Learning Disabilities: Theories, Diagnosis, and Teaching Strategies* 7th ed. Boston: Houghton Mifflin.

Lonigan, C. J., & Whitehurst, G. J. (1998). Relative efficacy of parent and teacher involvement in a shared-reading intervention for preschool children from low-income backgrounds. *Early Childhood Research Quarterly, 13,* 263–290.

Love, H. D., & Litton, F. W. (1994). *Teaching Reading to Disabled and Handicapped Learners.* Springfield, IL: Charles C. Thomas.

McCormick, S. (Ed.). (2003). *Instructing Students Who Have Literacy Problems.* Upper Saddle River, NJ: Pearson.

McNaughton, S. (1995). *Patterns of Emergent Literacy: Processes of Development and Transition.* Melbourne, VIC, Australia: Oxford University Press.

Moore, D. W., Bean, T. W., Birdyshaw, D., & Rycik, J. A. (1999). Adolescent literacy: A position statement. *Journal of Adolescent and Adult Literacy, 43*, 97–111.

Morrow, L. M., & Young, J. (1997). A family literacy program connecting school and home: Effects on attitude, motivation, and literacy achievement. *Journal of Educational Psychology, 89*, 736–742.

Nastasi, B. F., Moore, R. B., & Varjas, K. M. (2004). *School-Based Mental Health Services: Creating Comprehensive and Culturally Specific Programs.* Washington, D.C.: American Psychological Association.

National Research Council (2002). *Minority Students in Special and Gifted Education.* Washington, D.C.: National Academy Press.

Neuman, S. B. (1999). Creating continuity in early literacy: Linking home and school with a culturally responsive approach. In L. B. Gambrell, L. M. Morrow, S. B. Neuman, & M. Pressley (Eds.). *Best Practices in Literacy Instruction.* New York: Guilford Press.

Nistler, R. J., & Maiers, A. (1999). Exploring home-school connections. *Education and Urban Society, 32*, 3–17.

Pianta, R. C. (1990). Widening the debate on educational reform. Prevention as a viable alternative. *Exceptional Children, 56*, 306–313.

Pressley, M. (1999). *Reading Instruction That Works: The Case for Balanced Teaching.* New York: Guilford Press.

Rayner, K. (Ed.). (1992). *Eye Movements and Visual Cognition: Scene Perception and Reading.* New York: Springer-Verlag.

Rayner, K., & Pollatsek, A. (1989). *The Psychology of Reading.* Hillsdale, NJ: Erlbaum.

Roberts, J., Jurgens, J., & Burchinal, M. (2005). The role of home literacy practices in pre-school children's language and emergent literacy skills. *Journal of Speech, Language, and Hearing Research, 48*, 345–359.

Salinger, T. (2003). Helping older struggling readers. *Preventing School Failure, 47*, 79–85.

Shaywitz, S. E. (1998). Dyslexia. *New England Journal of Medicine, 338*, 307–312.

Shaywitz, S. E., Escobar, M. D., Shaywitz, B. A., & Fletcher, J. M. (1992). Evidence that dyslexia may represent the lower tail of a normal distribution of reading ability. *New England Journal of Medicine, 326*, 145–150.

Sheridan, S. M., & Kratochwill, T. R. (1992). Behavioral parent-teacher consultation: Conceptual and research considerations. *Journal of School Psychology, 30*, 117–139.

Sheridan, S. M., Kratochwill, T. R., & Bergan, J. R. (1996). *Conjoint Behavioral Consultation: A Procedural Manual.* New York: Plenum Press.

Shonnenschein, S., Baker, L., Serpell, R., & Schmidt, D. (2000). Reading as a source of entertainment: The importance of the home perspective for children's literacy development. In K. A. Roskos & J. F. Christie (Eds.), *Play and Literacy in Early Childhood: Research from Multiple Perspectives* (pp. 107–124). Mahwah, NJ: Erlbaum.

Shonnenschein, S., Brody, G., & Munsterman, K. (1996). The influence of family beliefs and practices on children's early reading development. In L. Baker, P. Afflerbach & D. Reinking (Eds.), *Developing Engaged Readers in School and Home Communities* (pp. 3–20). Mahwah, NJ: Erlbaum.

Snow, C. E., Burns, S., & Griffin, P. (1998). *Preventing Reading Difficulties in Young Children.* Washington, D.C.: National Academy Press.

Snow, C., & Tabors, P. (1996). Intergenerational transfer of literacy. In L. A. Benjamin & J. Lord (Eds.), *Family Literacy Directions in Research and Implications for Practice.* Washington, D.C.: Office of Educational Research and Improvement, U.S. Department of Education.

Snowling, M. J. (2000). *Dyslexia* 2nd ed. Malden, MA: Blackwell.

Stanovich, K. E. (1988). The right and the wrong places to look for the cognitive locus of reading disability. *Annals of Dyslexia, 38*, 154–177.

Stanovich, K. E. (1991). Discrepancy definitions of reading disability: Has intelligence led us astray? *Reading Research Quarterly, 26*, 7–29.

Stanovich, K. E. (1992). Speculations on the causes and consequences of individual differences in early reading acquisition. In P. Gough, L. Ehri & R. Trieman (Eds.), *Reading Acquisition* (pp. 307–342). Hillsdale, NJ: Erlbaum.

Torgesen, J. K. (2000). Individual responses in response to early interventions in reading: A lingering problem of treatment resisters. *Learning Disabilities Research & Practice, 15*, 55–64.

U.S. Immigration and Naturalization Service. (2002). Immigration Fact Sheet. Washington, D.C.: U.S. Department of Justice.

Vaughn, S., Linan-Thompson, S., & Hickman, P. (2003). Response to instruction as a means of identifying students with reading/learning disabilities. *Exceptional Children, 69*, 391–409.

Waldbart, A., Meyers, B., & Meyers, J. (2006). Invitations to families in an early literacy support program. *The Reading Teacher, 59*, 774–785.

Weigel, D. J., Martin, S. S., & Bennett, K. K. (2005). Ecological influences of the home and the child-care center on preschool-age children's literacy development. *Reading Research Quarterly, 40*, 204–233.

Welch, M., & Sheridan, S. M. (1995). *Educational Partnerships: Serving Children at Risk.* San Antonio, TX: Harcourt-Brace Jovanovich.

Witt, J., & Beck, R. (1999). *One-Minute Academic Functional Assessment and Interventions. "Can't Do it or Won't Do It."* Longmount, CO: Sopris West.

Wolf, M., & Bowers, P. G. (1999). The double-deficit hypothesis for the development of dyslexia. *Journal of Educational Psychology, 91*, 415–438.

Chapter 3

Assessment of Reading Performance That Is Linked to Targeting Reading Interventions

This chapter begins with a discussion about the pitfalls of using traditional methods of assessment that measure IQ or reading achievement discrepancies. It describes some of the assessment tools designed to target appropriate interventions: interviews, direct observations, curriculum-based measures, miscue analysis inventories, and informal reading inventories.

School psychologists and other educational consultants need to make school districts realize that, although IQ and achievement discrepancy methods have been used for many years to identify children with reading difficulties, they are not adequate means of identifying all children who experience reading difficulties and who are in need of intervention services (Lyon, Shaywitz, & Chhabra, 2004; Stanovich, 1991; Vellutino, Scanlon, & Lyon, 2000). This has been the case for young children especially. Some claim that in many instances children were not provided with appropriate types of interventions until they reached the age at which discrepancies between intellectual ability and academic achievement become apparent. However, even when discrepancies become apparent, these methods of assessment are not sufficient for assessing specific reading skill performance or for targeting appropriate reading instruction. Furthermore, students who struggle to obtain reading skills deserve appropriate types of assessment that are linked to the targeting and implementation of effective interventions. Several norm-referenced reading assessments are available, which are primarily used to compare a student's performance with his or her peers. Though these measures may have some diagnostic use for estimating reading skill delays compared with a normative sample, they tend not to provide sufficient information with regard to targeting specific skills for instruction purposes (Elliot & Fuchs, 1997). Advances in reading assessment are needed;

however, some methods and tools can be used to identify specific skill needs that are linked to targeting appropriate interventions. The assessments presented here are those that can be used to identify specific skill levels as well as to monitor progress in skill development. In other words, the measures described here assess specific reading skills, are used to determine where to begin instruction, and can be repeatable over time to measure students' progress during instruction. The following section describes a process for directly assessing reading performance. This process is derived in part from the work of Shapiro (2004).

DIRECT ASSESSMENT OF READING PERFORMANCE

Conducting a direct assessment of reading performance consists of the following steps: (1) obtaining some information about skill areas of concern through a consultation checklist form (i.e., referral type of form); (2) completing an in-depth interview with parents, teachers, and student; (3) conducting a systematic direct observation of student; and (4) administering reading performance assessments. School psychologists and other educational consultants can work collaboratively with educators in using these forms of assessment so that the individual student's reading skill levels are targeted for designing instruction.

Consultation Checklist Form

Before beginning an in-depth assessment, the school psychologist or other educational consultant may wish to administer a consultation checklist form to teachers or parents. This checklist form can be given to a teacher or a parent when a child is being referred for reading problems to the school psychologist or other educational consultants. An example of a consultation checklist form can be seen in Figure 3-1. A checklist may consist of a list of various reading skills, with places for the teacher or parent to mark whether or not the skill has been mastered. The next step would be to follow up with more in-depth interview questions.

Interviews With Parents, Teachers, and Student

When a student has been referred with reading problems, the school psychologist or educational consultant may begin the assessment process by conducting an interview with the student's teachers, the student, and the student's parent(s) or caregiver(s). Interviews can serve as a first step in the problem-solving process and can be used to formulate a hypothesis about the causes of the problem (Dawson, 2005). The interview should consist of questions that are aimed at gathering specific information with regard to a student's reading behaviors, including, for instance, the student's current reading skill levels.

The goal is to ascertain observable reading behaviors, such as "the student can read second grade and two months passages independently" and "the student has difficulty making one-to-one letter-sound correspondences of consonant-vowel-consonant phonogram words," not general observations such as "the student is reading below grade level" or "the student cannot process sounds."

Therefore, questioning needs to continue until the interviewer can ascertain the following:

- Whether students have obtained prereading skills, such as phoneme awareness and vocabulary.
- The grade level of text at which the student reads effortlessly, with some assistance, and with much assistance.
- The types of difficulties students are having with regard to oral word reading skills, such as the types of words (spelling patterns) they can read versus those they cannot read.
- The types of miscues (oral reading errors) students exhibit.
- The student's reading comprehension, such as types of meanings they get from text (literal and inferential).
- The strategies students use to read words and gain meaning from the text.
- Instructional methods and interventions that have been implemented with the student.
- Teacher, parent, and student expectations regarding reading performance.

Systematic Direct Observation of Engaged Reading Behaviors

Systematic direct observations of engaged reading behaviors can occur before or after an interview or both (Shapiro, 2004). The interview can serve to define the reading behaviors that are to be observed. Multiple, systematic observations are recommended. When the direct observation occurs before conducting an interview, the consultant can use the interview to get more information about the instructional materials, setting, and instructional delivery that may not have been directly apparent during the observation period. Observation after an interview can be used to observe certain targeted reading behaviors that may have been described during the interview.

Various types of direct observation can be used such as time-sampling, narration, and reading performance based assessments.

Time-Sampling Procedure

One form of a time-sampling procedure is the Behavior Observation of Students in Schools (appears in Shapiro, 2004). This measure uses momentary time-sampling procedures to observe active or passive engaged time spent in reading activities. Observation techniques that measure engaged time on reading tasks are important. At times, performance problems can be observed rather than skill problems. In other words, some children have the skills necessary to read proficiently but choose not to engage in the behavior, whereas other students have difficulty executing skills that would allow them to read proficiently, making it difficult to remain engaged in the activity.

Figure 3-1. *Consultation checklist for teachers who work with children with reading problems.*

CONSULTATION CHECKLIST OF READING PROBLEMS

The following questions have been designed to help determine which reading skills need to be further evaluated. Responses to these questions will be used in conjunction with other evaluative measures in order to gain a better understanding of academic functioning and to aid in the development of appropriate reading interventions.

Directions: Please answer the following questions, to the best of your knowledge, by checking the box in either the "Yes" or "No" column in each section.

Basic Literacy Skills

Can the student:	Yes	No
1. Name the letters of the alphabet?	☐	☐
2. Correctly identify all letter sounds? (e.g., B makes the /B/ sound)	☐	☐
3. Orally produce rhyming sounds and words?	☐	☐
4. Orally identify the first and last letter sounds in a spoken word?	☐	☐
5. Identify the medial sound in a word?	☐	☐
6. Blend sounds together to form a whole word? (e.g., /S/-/I/-/T/ becomes SIT)	☐	☐
7. Orally segment words into individual phonemes? (e.g., CAT becomes /C/-/A/-/T/)	☐	☐
8. Read one-syllable words?	☐	☐
9. Read multi-syllable words?	☐	☐
10. Make word analogies? (e.g., can read *pig* then can also read *wig*)	☐	☐
11. Use decoding skills to sound out unknown words?	☐	☐

Reading Fluency

Can the student:	Yes	No
1. Orally read most words accurately, effortlessly, and at a conversational pace within connected text?	☐	☐
2. Use proper vocal expression when reading orally? (e.g., varies appropriately with text and punctuation changes)	☐	☐
3. Use proper phrasing when reading orally? (e.g., pauses at commas, no run-on sentences)	☐	☐
4. Use proper vocal volume when reading orally? (e.g., not too quietly or loudly)	☐	☐

Vocabulary

Can the student:	Yes	No
1. Use age-appropriate vocabulary when speaking?	☐	☐
2. Define the majority of the words within an age- and grade-appropriate reading passage?	☐	☐
3. Interpret word meaning within the context of a reading passage?	☐	☐

Comprehension

Can the student:	Yes	No
1. Answer literal questions regarding the content of a reading passage?	☐	☐
2. Answer inferential questions regarding a reading passage?	☐	☐
3. Paraphrase or retell the content of a reading passage?	☐	☐
4. Summarize a reading passage (either orally or through writing)?	☐	☐
5. Accurately sequence events of a reading passage?	☐	☐
6. Identify cause-and-effect relationships within the content of a reading passage?	☐	☐
7. Make connections about events within the content of a reading passage?	☐	☐
8. Understand conceptual relationships within the content of a reading passage?	☐	☐

Additional Comments and/or Concerns

_____

_____

_____

_____

_____

_____

_____

_____

_____

_____

Systematic direct observation can also be conducted on the number of opportunities students are given to read during multiple class sessions. This type of observation not only focuses on the student but also focuses on the classroom instructional environment. It may be discovered, for instance, that students are provided with very few opportunities to be engaged in reading activities. This form of observation may also call attention to the types of reading activities that children are asked to engage in. For instance, children may be given many opportunities to complete workbook exercises but very few opportunities to read connected text. Systematic direct observations of reading behaviors can confirm or refute educators', parents', or students' judgment about their reading behaviors. Demaray and Elliot (1998) and Feinberg and Shapiro (2003) found that judgments using rating scales and other indirect ways of making judgments were not related strongly to how the student actually behaved. Perceptions of how the students are performing in reading are important from the standpoint of whether expectations of the student's ability are appropriate. However, consultants need to keep in mind that perceptions are not fact and need to be confirmed or disproved through direct observation of reading behavior.

Narration

Another form of observation would be to record a narrative of the reading behaviors observed during individual, small group, or large group oral reading instruction time. Anecdotal recording of reading behaviors should be used to supplement the information gathered using a time-sampling recording method. For instance, the strategies that children are using to orally read words or to comprehend text can be recorded in narrative form.

Reading Performance Assessment

Reading performance assessment is critical to obtaining precise information about the reading skills that children have and have not yet mastered. Reading performance assessment may include measures that address students' skills in reading words in isolation, reading words in connected text, and answering comprehension questions. A description of these types of reading measurement tools is provided here.

Word Attack Performance Assessment

A *word attack* skills assessment such as those described by Carnine, Silbert, Kame'enui, and Tarver (2004) can be used to assess word recognition performance when words are presented in isolation. Performance on this type of measure provides information that helps an examiner select passages at appropriate difficulty levels to be used when conducting oral reading accuracy and fluency assessments and comprehension assessment. A word attack assessment can also provide an indication of the phonic and structural elements that are known and unknown to the student. Words are presented in a list and are ordered according to phonic and structural elements. The phonic element corresponding to each word is written in parentheses on the examiner's copy. The student is asked to read the words on the list, and the examiner records responses as correct or incorrect. Incorrect responses are written down. The student has three seconds to read each word, and the test is discontinued when the student makes four consecutive incorrect responses.

Informal Reading Inventory Assessment

When teachers were surveyed, they found informal reading inventories and curriculum-based measures to be the most helpful for determining at what level students are reading and where to begin instruction (Cambell, 2001). According to Paris and Hoffman's (2004) research, informal reading inventories, coupled with miscue analysis, can provide an educator with a good estimate about an individual student's reading skill level and at about what level instruction should begin. Many well-developed informal reading inventories (IRIs) are available commercially. IRIs are a series of graded passages that are designed to be read orally as well as silently. Each grade-level passage contains one hundred to two hundred words. McCormick (2003) offers general guidelines for administering IRIs. Many IRIs have entry-level word lists that the students read, and the examiner selects a passage level depending on the number of words read accurately and inaccurately on the word lists. A tape recorder is used during oral reading of the passages to record types of oral reading errors (miscues) that are being made. The examiner may state a purpose for reading a certain passage and tells the student that comprehension questions will be asked after the passage is read. The passage is presented and the student is asked to read it either orally or silently. If the student orally reads the passage and comes to a word that he or she cannot read, the examiner may prompt the student by asking the student to use any familiar strategy to figure out how to read the word or to skip the word if he or she still cannot pronounce it after this prompt is given. If the student is asked to silently read the text, the examiner should remain in close view to make sure that the student is continuing to focus. In both types of testing, comprehension questions are asked after students read the passage, and their responses are tape-recorded. The number of questions answered correctly is recorded. The examiner later listens again to the tape recording of the oral reading and the students' answers to comprehension questions. Using a duplicate copy of the passage, the examiner records words read correctly and incorrectly as well as correct and incorrect responses to comprehension questions. Types of miscues are also recorded.

Various types of miscues include making substitutions, omissions, insertions, use of nonwords, word reversals, repetitions, self-corrections, hesitations, and ignored punctuation. A substitution may be saying the word *then* for the word *that*. Omissions and insertions are leaving out a word that is in the text or adding a word that is not there. The use of nonwords refers to substituting a nonsense word for a real word, such as *nuk* for *net*. Word reversal refers to pronouncing words backward, for instance saying the word *saw* as *was*. In repetition, students repeat the same word or phrase. Self-corrections are when students correct an error after making it. Hesitations are long pauses before the student pronounces a word. Students also may appear to have ignored punctuation, such as a comma, period, question mark, or explanation mark. The examiner uses specific marking procedures for recording various types of miscues. For instance, a word that is omitted may be circled. Hesitations may be represented by a dash between words in text.

By using informal reading inventories, the examiner can determine independent, instructional, and frustration levels. A passage is at a student's *independent* reading level when the student reads 96–100 percent of the words correctly and comprehends 90–100 percent of the text. A passage is at a student's *instructional* reading level when the student reads 90–95 percent of the words correctly and comprehends 70–89 percent of the text. A passage is at a student's *frustration* level when the student is able to read below 90 percent of the words correctly and comprehends below 70 percent of the text. Passages are administered until the examiner determines when the student has reached his or her frustration level.

In the past, informal reading inventories were used to assess oral reading accuracy. Today, many educators use informal reading inventories to measure accuracy, rate, and prosody (Paris & Hoffman, 2004). The following is a list of commercially produced reading inventories:

- *Reading Inventory for the Classroom*, 4th edition (preprimer through 12th grade), by E. Sutton Flynt and Robert B. Cooter; Merrill/Prentice Hall (2001).
- *Basic Reading Inventory*, 8th edition (preprimer through 12th grade), by Jerry L. Johns; Kendall/Hunt (2001).
- *Analytical Reading Inventory*, 7th edition (primer through 9th grade), by Mary Lynn Woods and Alden J. Moe; Prentice Hall (2002).
- *Classroom Reading Inventory*, 9th edition (preprimer through 8th grade), by Nicholas J. Silvaroli and Warren H. Wheelock; McGraw-Hill (2001).

Curriculum-Based Assessment

The next step is to assess students' reading performance using curriculum-based measures of oral reading passages. Curriculum-based measures have been validated as time-efficient, standardized methods for identifying oral reading fluency performance and for monitoring progress in achieving oral reading fluency goals (Deno, 2003; Shinn, 1998). Curriculum-based measures can be used in conjunction with and to supplement informal reading inventories with miscue analysis. Once a student's instructional level of reading has been determined, curriculum-based oral reading measures can be used to assess progress in reading instructional-level passages and to determine when instructional-level passages become independent-level passages for readers.

The beauty of using curriculum-based reading measures is that measurement is repeatable over time, so progress can be detected and instructional decisions can be made sooner rather than later. Passages can be selected from basal or literature-based text in the classroom. Readability estimates can be calculated to determine the reading grade level of the text. A student is given one minute to orally read the passage while the examiner records the words read correctly and those read incorrectly. Three passages are typically administered to the student in this fashion, so that a mean oral reading fluency performance can be derived. Comprehension questions pertaining to the contents in the passage can be administered after the timed oral reading of a passage. Performance on curriculum-based measures informs teachers about when to make changes in instruction before students are administered statewide performance-based reading tests. McGlinchey and Hixson (2004) found that curriculum-based measures predicted performance on statewide performance-based assessments. Therefore, the use of curriculum-based measures for progress monitoring provides a good indication of how students will eventually perform on state reading assessments.

A student's comprehension rate can be measured with the use of curriculum-based passages that include a number of comprehension questions (literal and inferential). Skinner, Neddenriep, Bradley-Klug, and Zieman (2002) describe a method for calculating comprehension rate. The student is asked to read a passage and is timed with regard to how long (in minutes and seconds) he or she takes to read the passage. Afterward, the student is asked an even number of literal and inferential comprehension questions without referring back to the passage. The number of correct responses is recorded and a percentage of accurate responses is calculated. The percentage is then multiplied by sixty seconds and divided by the number of seconds required to read the passage. This numerical figure is the rate at which the student is comprehending text for every minute the passage is read. Additionally, it maybe important to calculate the actual rate of responses to questions by multiplying the number of questions answered correctly by sixty seconds and dividing by the total amount of time it takes to answer a set of questions. Latency measures may also be used to record the length of time that elapses before executing an oral or written response.

Early Reading Assessment

When it has been determined that children do not possess many word attack skills, an assessment that measures prereading skills is needed to determine if the student has the prerequisite skills necessary to make letter-sound correspondences. The Dynamic Indicators of Basic Early Literacy Skills (DIBELS; Good & Kaminski, 2002) is a measurement system that assesses early literacy, fluency, and comprehension skills. DIBELS was developed by researchers from the University of Oregon. The assessment materials and methods are free and can be downloaded from a website, http://dibels.uoregon.edu. Comparisons can be made to other students' performance using a large national database, which is also available on the website. School districts can obtain quarterly reports on their pupils' performance for a minimal fee.

DIBELS measures phoneme segmentation fluency, initial sound fluency, letter-naming fluency, blending sounds, oral reading fluency, and retellings. All skills are assessed in a standardized way. The measures come in multiple forms and the administration time is brief, making it possible to assess performance levels for many students rather quickly. On the phoneme segmentation fluency measure, students are asked to segment all the sounds in a whole word. Each sound segment of a word is scored as either correct or incorrect. An accuracy score is derived by recording the total correct sounds segmented divided by the total items administered. Fluency is recorded by calculating the total sounds correctly segmented per minute.

For initial sound fluency, the student is required to tell the examiner the sound a word starts with after the examiner orally presents a word. The total correct initial sounds divided by the total sounds administered is calculated, as well as the total correct per minute.

Oral reading fluency measures consist of the examiner asking the students to read a passage for one minute and then recording the words read accurately per minute. Retelling fluency involves asking the student to retell a passage after a one-minute oral reading of the passage. This is administered to students who could read at least ten words correctly during one-minute timed oral reading of passages. After the one-minute reading, the student is prompted to tell the examiner all about what was just read. The examiner records the number of words the student says correctly. The student is given one minute to retell what he or she has read. Each word retold from the story is counted as correct as long as the student appears as if he or she is retelling the story and not something else. It is not always apparent in the retelling whether the student has gained meaning from the story.

In relatively recent years, the DIBELS has been expanded to include assessment materials not only for primary-grade children but also for intermediate grades. Users are encouraged to visit the website periodically to determine if these measures are being expanded to include grades beyond intermediate elementary-grade levels. Other comprehension measures may need to be administered to ascertain if children are getting meaning from the text. Other types of curriculum-based measures can be obtained from Edformation (www.edformation.com) and Intervention Central (www.interventioncentral.org).

MAKING EVIDENCE-BASED DECISIONS

Once the data are gathered and specific problems have been identified, appropriate goals should be established with regard to a student's reading performance. The next decision that needs to be made is the selection of evidence-based instructional methods to be implemented to help the student meet desired reading performance goals. Interventions should be selected based on the skill needs identified and the identified goals. For instance, assessment data may indicate that the student orally reads words accurately but does not read words accurately and quickly. In that case, the intervention of choice would be one that improves fluency, such as timed repeated oral readings of passages (see chapter 5 for a description of this method). In other words, the intervention is selected to match the reading skill needs of the student or class of students. Perhaps assessment using curriculum-based measures determined that over half of the students in the class need to improve their fluency, and that therefore repeated readings need to be implemented with the entire class. Thus, the key to making evidence-based decisions is to base instruction interventions on data from assessments that are directly linked to targeted skill levels and types of instruction.

WHAT CAN SCHOOL PSYCHOLOGISTS AND OTHER EDUCATIONAL CONSULTANTS DO?

- Advocate for the use of assessment methods that directly target specific skill functioning levels and ones which are linked to selecting interventions.
- Gather data from multiple stakeholders when possible and in multiple settings.

- Use both accuracy and rate measures to more effectively identify students' instructional needs.
- Monitor students' progress through the use of direct assessments.
- Make instructional decisions based on data obtained from direct assessments.

SUMMARY POINTS

- Direct assessment of reading performance involves interviews with students, systematic observations, word attack assessments, and reading performance assessments.
- An interview should consist of questions that are directed at obtaining specific information about a student's reading behavior, including current skills and levels of functioning.
- Momentary time sampling is an effective way of conducting a systematic direct observation. Recording a narrative about the behaviors and events observed can supplement findings from a time-sampling procedure.
- Assessing students' word attack skills when words are presented in isolation provides useful information about students' reading skills without using context clues.
- Information gathered from informal reading inventories and miscue analysis can help teachers make decisions about students' *independent, instructional,* and *frustration* reading levels.
- Curriculum-based measurements are useful for assessing accuracy and rate (oral reading fluency).

QUESTIONS FOR DISCUSSION

1. Discuss how the use of traditional methods of intelligence and achievement assessment may not be ideal for identifying children with reading difficulties.
2. What is the primary aim of conducting interviews with parents, teachers, and the student?
3. Discuss how different types of direct observation, such as assessments based on time-sampling, narration, and reading performance, can be used together to gather comprehensive information about students' reading behavior and performance.
4. How are students' independence, instructional, and frustration levels determined? Why is this important?
5. Briefly describe how a student's performance on a DIBELS measure may lead to the selection of a specific evidence-based instructional intervention.

REFERENCES

Campbell, M. B. (2001). Inquiry into reading assessment: Teachers' perceptions of effective practices. *Reading Horizons, 42,* 1–20.

Carnine, D. W., Silbert, J., Kame'enui, E. J., & Tarver, S. G. (Eds.). (2004). *Direct Reading Instruction* (4th ed.). Upper Saddle River, NJ: Pearson.

Dawson, P. (2005). Using interviews to understand different perspectives in school-related problems. In R. Brown-Chidsey (Ed.), *Assessment for Intervention* (pp. 155–174). New York: Guilford Press.

Demaray, M. K., & Elliot, S. N. (1998). Teachers' judgements of students' academic functioning: A comparison of actual and predicted performances. *School Psychology Quarterly, 13,* 8–24.

Deno, S. L. (2003). Developments in curriculum-based measurement. *Journal of Special Education, 37,* 184–192.

Elliot, S. N., & Fuchs, L. S. (1997). The utility of curriculum-based measurement and performance assessment as alternatives to traditional intelligence and achievement tests. *School Psychology Review, 26,* 224–233.

Feinberg, A. B., & Shapiro, E. S. (2003). Accuracy of teacher judgments in predicting oral reading fluency. *School Psychology Quarterly, 18,* 52–65.

Good, R. H., & Kaminski, R. A. (Eds.). (2002). *Dynamic Indicators of Basic Early Literacy Skills* (6th ed.). Eugene, OR: Institute for the Development of Educational Achievement. Retrieved, October 5, 2005, from http://dibels.uoregon.edu

Lyon, G. R., Shaywitz, S. E., & Chhabra, V. (2004). Evidence-based reading skill policy in the United States: How scientific research informs instructional practice. In D. Ravitch (Ed.), *Brookings Papers on Education Policy: 2005* (pp. 198–216). Washington, D.C.: Brookings.

McCormick, S. (Ed.). (2003). *Instructing Students Who Have Literacy Problems.* Upper Saddle River, NJ: Merrill/Prentice Hall.

McGlinchey, M. T., & Hixson, M. D. (2004). Using curriculum-based measurement to predict performance on state assessments in reading. *School Psychology Review, 33,* 193–203.

Paris, S. G., & Hoffman, J. V. (2004). Reading assessments in kindergarten through third grade: Findings from the center for the improvement of early reading achievement. *Elementary School Journal, 105,* 199–217.

Shapiro, E. S. (2004). *Academic Skills Problems Workbook (Rev. ed.).* New York: Guilford Press.

Shinn, M. R. (Ed.). (1998). *Advanced Applications of Curriculum-Based Measurement*. New York: Guilford Press.

Skinner, C. H., Neddenriep, C. E., Bradley-Klug, K. L., & Zieman, J. M. (2002). Advances in curriculum-based measurement: Alternative rate measures for assessing reading skills in pre- and advanced readers. *Behavior Analyst Today, 3*, 270–281.

Stanovich, K. E. (1991). Discrepancy definition of reading disability: Has intelligence led us astray? *Reading Research Quarterly, 26*, 7–29.

Vellutino, F. R., Scanlon, D. M., & Lyon, G. R. (2000). Differentiating between difficult to remediate and readily remediated poor readers: More evidence against the IQ-achievement discrepancy definition for reading disability. *Journal of Learning Disabilities, 33*, 223–238.

SECTION TWO

Evidence-Based Reading Interventions

This section contains four chapters. The first chapter, chapter 4, describes several evidence-based principles and components of effective teaching that can be used with several intervention techniques, strategies, and programs and across various reading skills. These components are discussed in the first chapter of this section to highlight the critical role these principles play in implementing particular techniques or programs. Executing these principles can enhance the quality of a particular technique and may be the very element that produces desired reading performance outcomes.

Chapters 5 and 6 describe specific reading techniques, strategies, and programs at the word reading and comprehension levels. Evidence-based interventions and guidelines for selecting interventions are discussed at the beginning of chapter 5. The chapter also presents several techniques, strategies, and interventions for word reading, including phonic analysis and fluency interventions. In most cases, descriptions of the materials, procedures, and research supporting the use of the interventions are presented.

Chapter 6 describes comprehension interventions, which include interventions for developing vocabulary, obtaining factual information, forming conceptual relationships, and making inferences. Materials, procedures, and research supporting the use of these interventions are also presented.

Chapter 7 presents methods for evaluating the effectiveness of interventions using functional or experimental analyses. Response-to-intervention models are also discussed within an experimental analysis framework. This final chapter in the book is critical for meeting the individual needs of students who experience challenges in learning to read and becoming proficient readers.

Chapter 4
Effective Teaching Principles of Reading

Often, teachers and parents will ask school psychologists and educational consultants to suggest techniques or programs they can use to teach reading skills to children. Techniques and programs alone do not help children learn reading skills. Generally speaking, effective instruction enables students to achieve competency and generalize learning more efficiently than they would on their own or with less than effective instruction (Fredrick & Hummel, 2004). Thus, the most critical aspect of instruction is the use of effective principles of teaching, which can then be applied while using just about every technique or program.

ELEVEN HIGHLY EFFECTIVE PRINCIPLES OF INSTRUCTION

The effective principles of teaching include building on schemata and prerequisite skills, conducting a task analysis of skills, being explicit and direct when teaching skills, demonstrating and modeling skills, engaging children actively in reading, providing many opportunities to read and practice on reading skills, providing positive reinforcement for effort and shaping skills for successful reading performance, providing feedback, scaffolding skills, teaching to mastery, and promoting generalization of skills. In this chapter, each principle is discussed separately, but the discussion of many of these concepts will overlap. These principles can be used and gradually faded throughout students' reading skill development as they encounter new challenges. Rosenshine (1995) provided a seminal review of research on the effectiveness of these principles and components of teaching reading. In subsequent chapters in this book, these principles are also embedded in discussions about instructional techniques and programs.

Building on Schemata and Prerequisite Skills

The foundation on which new knowledge or skills are built is referred to as schemata. *Schemata* are prior knowledge or background information. Researchers can predict how well students will obtain meaning from new content or learn new skills by assessing their prior knowledge (Gambrell & Massoni, 1999). When children learn to read words, they may activate their prior knowledge about the word in their receptive and expressive language repertoires. When children read a section of text for the first time, they likely will activate their prior knowledge to help them make sense of the new content in the text or to make predictions about the content they are reading, such as predicting what might happen next in a story (Pressley, 1999). However, not all children automatically activate their schemata when they encounter new content or skills. Educators can help students build on their experiences and background knowledge when they introduce new content or skills. Building on students' prior knowledge and experiences guides their learning, helping to ease their way and motivating them to engage in reading new content or learning new skills.

What is prior knowledge? Prior knowledge could be students' acquired knowledge from experiences at home, in their communities, or on a trip they took. Educators who learn about their students and their experiences can relate new content and skills to the knowledge in their students' repertoires. For example, teachers can ask children if they have ever been to a beach and ask what they saw there and what activities they did before reading a passage about events that occur at a beach. Teachers can also conduct interviews with students to discover their background and their interests. If children do not have prior knowledge through experiences or otherwise in relation to the new content, teachers need to take advantage of the moment and be responsive to students' needs by providing them with the prerequisite knowledge, which may involve introducing concepts before those concepts are read in a story or passage.

Prior knowledge can also be skills that have been previously learned. These skills often are foundational skills or basic skills from which other skills are derived. These are referred to as prerequisite skills. Teachers may observe that children often forget previously learned skills when new skills are introduced. Children may forget how to read some words taught a week ago when they are taught how to read new words. For example, children may forget to read *fat* when they learn how to read *fate*. In this instance, they may read the word *fat* as *fate*. It is critical that each lesson begin by reviewing previously taught content or skills so that students are building on previously learned skills rather than replacing them with newly learned skills. Often, this means reviewing and or interspersing previously taught content and skills as a prerequisite for teaching new content and skills.

Conducting Task Analysis

How instruction is sequenced is very important. For reading instruction to be effective, reading skills need to be learned as a progression of skills. Task analysis involves ordering those skills in terms of a step-by-step progression for completing a particular task (Swanson & Hoskyn, 1998; Vaughn, Gersten, & Chard, 2000). According to Hummel, Venn, &

Gunter (2004), teachers can conduct task analysis by listing the steps in completing a task or learning a skill. Teachers should analyze tasks into first, second, and third steps and so forth so they are aware of the prerequisite skills students need to learn before higher, more advanced skills are taught. Too often, educators assume that children know some of the very basic skills or have mastered some of the basic steps, because these skills seem so automatic. These assumptions are made at every grade level but especially as children progress beyond the first-grade level. For instance, second- and third-grade teachers may assume that children have acquired basic one-to-one letter-sound correspondence for basic consonant-vowel-consonant (CVC) patterned words (e.g., CVC words as in *cup, dip*), but in fact students may not have mastered these basic reading skills because of a lack of appropriate instruction or opportunities to practice these skills.

Once teachers have analyzed tasks into specific orderly steps, they can assess children's performance, that is, their successful completion and mastery of each step. Assessment can help teachers determine whether they should move on to teaching the next step so students can complete the task. To assess whether children have mastered the steps, the teacher needs to have defined them in terms of students' overt behaviors in performing the step (Hummel, Venn, & Gunter, 2004). For instance, if the objective is for students to learn to read vowel sounds in words, educators may state, "students will correctly read the short vowel sound of /a/ in CVC patterned words."

Using Explicit and Direct Instruction

The term *explicit* means stated in detail and not merely implied. Therefore, reading instruction that is explicit means clearly describing the skill that is being taught and teaching it as described. If short vowel sounds are the teaching objective, then teachers need to make statements such as "Today we are going to learn how to read short vowel sounds beginning with the short vowel sound /a/." Teaching the short vowel sound in detail means having children read words that have the short vowel sound /a/ and also having them discriminate or identify words with short /a/ sounds from other words with short vowel sounds other than /a/ and among words with long /a/ vowel sounds. Teaching short vowel sounds in detail also means teaching children several words with short /a/ sounds so they can generalize to reading other words with short /a/ sounds in them. It is also important to teach words that have an /a/ in them, but the sound may be either a silent or a long /a/ sound. The National Reading Panel report (2000) indicated that favorable reading achievement outcomes are evident in children who have received explicit instruction on reading skills especially for those individuals who enter school with limited literacy experiences.

Essentially, to make reading instruction explicit, teachers need to teach skills directly. When most educators see the term *direct instruction*, they think of the program developed by Englemann and Bruner, (1988) (discussed in chapter 5 of this book). For now, the focus will be on direct instruction as a principle of effective teaching. When instruction is direct, it includes all of the effective teaching components (i.e., task analysis, demonstration, modeling, feedback, opportunities to respond and practice, reinforcement, shaping, scaffolding, teaching to mastery, and promotion of generalization) that are discussed in this chapter.

Educators who teach skills directly do not assume that children will implicitly or indirectly learn reading skills. When phonics, or making letter-sound correspondences, were not taught directly in many classrooms across the United States, several students, especially those that were most at risk of not learning reading skills, did not develop as proficient readers. Several of these classrooms applied a language-arts curriculum that was considered "meaning-based" rather than "code-emphasis based." Gaining meaning from text is certainly important; however, meaning cannot be derived from text if children do not know how to read or decode printed words in text. Assuming that children would learn decoding skills by merely being asked to read to gain meaning and comprehend text resulted in many nonreaders or children with very limited reading skills. Direct instruction is often associated with teaching very basic skills, but direct instruction can and should be used to teach complex skills such as reading comprehension as well (Baumann, 1984). In fact, complex skills are achievable for most children regardless of cognitive ability if those skills are broken down into steps (task analysis) and each step is taught directly. When skills are taught directly, students know what they are expected to learn and how they are expected to perform.

School psychologists and other educational consultants will encounter educators who are not knowledgeable about empirical findings and who deny the importance of research findings that clearly support teaching reading skills directly to children. Some educators claim that direct instruction of reading skills is not really teaching children how to read. Many of these educators have been trained to teach reading using a "whole language" or "constructivist" approach, which emphasizes the notion that children will construct meaning for themselves. However, research has taught us that many children do not learn skills or "pick up" on decoding skills by simply constructing meaning from text (National Reading Panel, 2000). Reading is not natural. Most children do not learn how to read on their own or with minimal guidance. Therefore, claims that direct instruction methods do not teach children how to read could not be further from the truth. Children have a better chance or more ample opportunities to learn to read if reading skills are taught directly. Thus, high quality reading instruction is instruction that is direct and systematic in which skills taught and learned build upon other skills and can be applied in multiple contexts (Carnine, Silbert, Kame'enui, & Tarver, 2004).

Demonstrating and Modeling Skills

Demonstration and modeling of skills are very important components of effective instruction. Although the terms may be used synonymously, modeling can be distinguished from demonstration. Modeling is performing an action or exhibiting a behavior for others to imitate. Demonstration involves showing someone how to perform an action or behavior by describing or explaining that action or behavior while it is occurring.

Modeling literacy behaviors is critical. It is important for children to see their parents, relatives, older siblings, peers, and teachers reading. Children have increased their reading accuracy by observing a fluent reader engaged in reading (McCurdy, Cundari, & Lentz, 1990). Children tend to do what they observe. Even young children who cannot yet decode print may imitate others or pretend to read print on a page by moving their eyes and head left to right as they look at and turn the pages of a book. In these respects, modeling is considered to be indirect instruction, or as referred to by some, incidental learning (Orelove, 1982).

A modeling strategy that has proved to be effective is listening while reading (Daly, Chafouleas, & Skinner, 2005). This has also been referred to as *listening passage preview* or *assisted reading*. During listening passage preview exercises, students may listen to a teacher or capable peer read a passage or listen to a tape-recorded reading of a passage. While the students are listening, they are following along and reading the passage silently. This procedure has been effective for improving oral reading fluency skills and comprehension for children with disabilities (Daly & Martens, 1994; Hale et al., 2005; Skinner, Cooper, & Cole, 1997). According to Daly, Chafouleas, et al. (2005), the best application of the listening passage preview modeling procedure is for the model (e.g., the teacher or prerecorded reader) to read the passage at a slow enough rate, but with proper rhythm and expression, so that children can easily follow along (Skinner, Logan, Robinson, & Robinson, 1997).

Although modeling reading behavior, in general, is critical and has certainly been found to be effective, it may not be sufficient for helping children learn to read. Educators and parents cannot assume that children will learn how to perform skills through observation (listening and seeing) alone. When a skill is new to a learner, educators need to go beyond mere modeling of the skill and demonstrate how to perform that skill.

Demonstrating how to read is a form of explicit instruction. In demonstration, the instructor describes or explains an action or behavior while they are doing it. When teachers demonstrate how to read, they vocalize the steps or processes they are performing. For instance, during an oral storybook reading activity a teacher may tell the students that she is opening a book to the first page of the book and is going to read the entire line of print beginning on the top line at the far left side of the page until she comes to the end of the line; then she will return to the far left side of the page again to read the first word on the second line. As she comes to a word such as *cat*, she may say that the word begins with the letter "c" so she will pronounce this letter as /c/. The next letter in the word is "a" and so will make the /a/ sound, and the last letter is "t" so she will make the /t/ sound. Then she explains that she will blend these sounds together to say the whole word, *cat*. After the teacher demonstrates how to read the page in the book, she may ask the students to try and read the page.

According to Skinner, Logan, et al. (1997), demonstration can serve as a prompt or cue to invite a response or to provide feedback after a response has been received. In the former example, demonstration served as a prompt to have the children read the story. As children attempt to read a page in the story, they may read words incorrectly or not at all. When this happens, educators may demonstrate how to read the words as a way of providing children with corrective feedback.

Actively Engaging Children and Providing Opportunities to Respond

Allocating time for reading during the school day and at home is essential but still not sufficient. Allocating time to read does not guarantee that reading is actually occurring during that time. It is important that students be actively engaged in reading in a meaningful way (Gettinger & Siebert, 2002). "Active engagement means that the students behave with respect to the things that are being taught" (Slocum, 2004, p. 89). Meaningful ways of being actively engaged in reading may include having many opportunities to perform a reading skill, such as orally reading a passage in a book, receiving feedback from the instructor on performance while reading, performing the reading skill after feedback has been provided, and self-monitoring reading skill performance.

Active engagement in reading can consist of covert as well as overt behaviors (Skinner, Pappas, & Davis, 2005). Covert reading behaviors are not easy to observe as they likely occur during silent reading activities. Covert behaviors may involve checking for understanding by silently previewing, vocalizing (paraphrasing or reciting), reviewing, questioning, predicting, and summarizing the content presented in text.

Overt reading behaviors are easier to observe and measure, making them more likely to be reinforced (Skinner, Pappas, & Davis, 2005). Overt reading behaviors may involve reading aloud, answering comprehension questions orally or in writing, choral responding during reading lessons, and monitoring one's own performance by recording responses in writing.

Providing many opportunities to respond (both overt and covert responses) increases the likelihood that students will receive extended practice of skills, a critical component of effective reading instruction (Swanson, 2001). Consultants need to work with teachers to ensure that plenty of opportunities to read are provided to students. When instructors are teaching reading skills that are new to learners, they need to make sure they are also providing students with many opportunities to practice the skills that are taught. Novice readers, in particular, need plenty of opportunities to orally read to their instructors and receive feedback on their performance. Some reading techniques and programs build in opportunities to respond, such as response cards, repeated readings, and DISTAR. These techniques and programs will be discussed in subsequent chapters in this section.

Providing Repeated Exposure to and Practice Reading

Providing students with opportunities to read is critical. It is also critical that teachers provide several opportunities for students to make the same response as well as by repeating the instruction several times or providing several exposures to the same content so that students are taught repeatedly until they make correct responses effortlessly (Slocum, 2004). Some students will need more repetitions than others, so teachers may need to adjust the number of repeated exposures to reading content and repeated instruction on specific reading skills to meet the diverse needs of the students in the class. The amount of repeated practice depends on the characteristics of the words (level of abstraction or how similar the words are to those that students have acquired). According to McCormick (2003), children in the early phases of word learning development (despite their chronological age) need more exposure and opportunities to practice reading the same words in multiple contexts than children in later phases of development. Children in later phases of word learning development draw upon word attack strategies and skills they have learned as they have progressed through the phases.

Research on repeated reading lessons have substantiated the necessity of repeated exposures, repeated opportunities to read, and repeated instruction on improving students' reading acquisition and reading rates (see Rasinski, 1990, for a review). Children with greater needs, such as those with mental retardation or learning disabilities, need more exposures and more opportunities to read than children who are developing reading skills at a typical rate (McCormick, 2003).

Giving Positive Reinforcement and Shaping Successful Reading

When something is reinforced, it is strengthened, and when it is not reinforced, it is weakened and may become extinct (Skinner, 1958). Therefore, reading skills are strengthened when they are reinforced and weakened if not used at all when they are not reinforced (Carnine, Silbert, Kame'enui, & Tarver, 2004). Reinforcement as a consequence of a behavior such as reading serves to increase the likelihood of the behavior (reading) occurring in the future. Pleasure or knowledge that one derives from reading is considered to be a "natural" reinforcer because it increases the likelihood that one will continue to engage in this behavior. Natural reinforcers are considered to be the least intrusive because they require minimal resources outside the context of the activity itself (e.g., reading a fiction novel for pleasure). Children who have difficulty learning to read or who have had a history of disappointments and failures in their attempts to read may need more intrusive reinforcers such as tokens, activities, and verbal reinforcers. These types of positive reinforcers may be given when children are making efforts to read or when they read successfully. Reinforcing efforts to learn to read is very important for a novice reader or a reader who has experienced difficulty with this skill.

Positive reinforcers can be delivered in successive approximations as a way to shape reading accurately and quickly. For instance, children may be given a reinforcer such as a sticker or praise for sounding out the first letter of a word and then provided with a reinforcer for sounding out the last letter in a word and then the middle letter or letters in a word. As students become more proficient at sounding out letters in words and reading words, reinforcers are given intermittently, such as after every two to three letters are sounded out, and gradually faded out to being delivered after an entire word is read. Eventually, a reinforcer is provided for every three to four words read fluently and then provided for reading an entire sentence, then a paragraph, and when a book is completed, and so forth. When children begin to read effortlessly and are able to derive meaning from text, these tangible, token, and verbal types of reinforcers are likely to be replaced with natural ones as the need for conditioned reinforcers decreases and as natural reinforcers, such as reading for entertainment and information (knowledge), increase. Thus, shaping reading skills means reinforcing reading behaviors in successive approximations until the desired goal is achieved.

Many educators and school policy makers gravely underestimate and even devalue the use of reinforcement. Many educators fear that children will not become self-motivated to perform tasks if extrinsic rewards or reinforcers are provided. Additionally, some educators feel that children should not be reinforced for behaviors they are expected to exhibit (Skinner, Pappas, & Davis, 2005). These educators essentially fail to apply their knowledge about human development (behavior) while educating for content and skills.

Human behavior is governed by antecedents (what comes before the behavior) and consequences (what comes after the behavior) (Skinner, 1958). Reinforcers are consequences, and some are delayed and others are immediate. Adults work for conditioned reinforcers such as money so they can exchange them for unconditioned reinforcers such as food. Diligent and high-quality work results in positive evaluations that transform into promotions or salary increases for many professionals.

Children may experience both immediate and delayed reinforcers when they engage in the act of reading. Verbal praise, special activities (playing a game), or tangibles can be chosen by students and delivered immediately or a few days after children read a certain number of words in a story. Immediate and delayed rewards can be experienced naturally for children who read often and widely. These children, for instance, will not only develop vocabulary and obtain information at that moment for immediate purposes but may also answer questions on college entrance exams in the future or learn content material more quickly and easily, reducing their amount of study time during their college years. Therefore, it is important for consultants to work with educators to shape students' reading behaviors—by reinforcing successive approximations of immediate reading achievement goals—so that students' future goals are more likely to be realized. Educators can do much with regard to establishing a strong history of systematic reinforcement for children so that a snowballing effect of lifelong positive reading behavior occurs.

Giving Feedback

Feedback on student reading performance is another critical instructional principle that leads to improved reading performance (Pany & McCoy, 1988). Feedback allows students to regulate their reading behaviors or performance. It lets students know, for instance, that they are or are not reading at an appropriate rate. Feedback can come in the form of verbal praise for successful performance or for efforts (successive approximations) to successful performance. When feedback is in the form of verbal praise, it is considered to be a type of conditioned reinforcer. Feedback can also be in the form of correcting a mistake or error. This is often called corrective feedback or error correction. For instance, when a child says the word *can* for *cane*, the teacher may provide corrective feedback by saying "That word is *cane* because it has an 'e' at the end of the word."

Feedback can be immediate or delayed. Immediate feedback, for instance, occurs when children are reading a passage and an instructor or peer corrects them as they encounter words they cannot read. Delayed feedback occurs, for example, after children finish reading the entire passage and then words that were read incorrectly are recorded and corrected by the instructor. Some research has revealed that immediate corrective feedback is more effective for helping students improve their reading performance than delayed feedback (Barbetta, Heron, & Heward, 1993; Barbetta, Heward, Bradley, & Miller, 1994). Children can be encouraged to check their own reading performance if passages or words are prerecorded on a tape or on some technological device and they can check their reading against the recorded version. Feedback guides students to read accurately and helps them regulate and monitor their reading performance. Corrective feedback, in general, has been proven to be effective. However, Rasinski and Hoffman (2003), feel that the research is still inconclusive in regard to determining the most effective types of corrective feedback (that is, immediate versus delayed).

Scaffolding Skills

In laymen's terms, a scaffold is generally referred to as a temporary platform that workmen use to work efficiently up off the ground, such as when completing construction of a house. Scaffolding in education is providing temporary support to children when they cannot perform reading skills independently and gradually fading that support as children learn to read on their own. This has been found to contribute to improved reading performance (Swanson & Hoskyn, 1998). Scaffolding can include providing prompts (guided practice), giving feedback, providing supportive materials, demonstrating, modeling, and shaping through reinforcement for successive approximations. According to Carnine et al. (2004), scaffolded assistance (guiding by prompting or cueing students to use strategies and problem-solving skills) is provided to students in a way that helps them assume more responsibility for their learning as they advance to achieving higher-order skills. For example, a teacher who provides scaffolded assistance may not supply the correct reading of a word when an error is made but instead may provide a prompt, such as "Examine the word carefully and tell me what sound it begins with," or use analogies to help students read words, such as "This word sounds a lot like…." Scaffolding or guided practice can be embedded within the instructional materials themselves, such as when vowels are written in bold-faced print to teach children to read vowel sounds.

Teaching to Mastery

An effective teacher is similar to a coach of an athletic team. Effective teachers teach to mastery just as a coach trains his players to win. Teaching reading skills to mastery means teaching until children read at proficient levels. Proficient means reading effortlessly and fluently and gaining meaning from the content. Establishing criterion levels of performance helps professionals determine whether goals or mastery have been achieved. Criterion levels can change (increase or decrease) depending on how well students are progressing toward mastery. Criterion levels of performance may have to be reduced a bit if the level is not achievable in a reasonable period of time and then raised again when the performance rate increases. Consultants need to help educators teach for mastery to ensure that reading achievement goals are accounted for and met.

Promoting Generalization of Skills

Generalization refers to giving the same response (reading a particular word) in the presence of stimuli (the printed word in a sentence) that are similar to a stimulus in which the response was learned (the printed word on a flashcard). Educators can promote generalization of skills by creating activities that require children to perform the same reading skill in multiple contexts. For instance, educators want children to read words in isolation as well as in a passage of a story. For example, the word *stop* is seen alone, such as on a street sign, and with other words, such as in a story. Children must know how to read this word in and out of connected text. Teaching using multiple exposures to the same word and plenty of opportunities to read the same word leads to overlearning, or practicing mastered skills in additional trials ("over and over"). The result is the student performs the skills much more accurately at a later time (Bahrick, Bahrick, Bahrick, & Bahrick, 1993). Overlearning not only leads to maintaining reading skills but also facilitates generalization of reading skills (McCormick, 2003). Thus, teaching skills to mastery increases the likelihood that children will generalize skills to a variety of reading situations (Daly, Chafouleas, et al., 2005).

TEACHING RON TO READ FLUENTLY USING EFFECTIVE TEACHING PRINCIPLES

The teacher checked out the book from the school library because she was interested in finding a book written at Ron's instructional reading level. She also wanted one that he would be highly interested in, and she discovered after talking to Ron that he plays baseball and watches the game on television. The story was about a baseball player. Before Ron was asked to read a story on his own, he listened and followed along in his book as Mrs. Yoder, his teacher, read the story. Mrs. Yoder demonstrated the use of word-decoding strategies as she encountered newly introduced vocabulary concepts in the text. She then provided a tape-recorded reading of the story and asked Ron to listen to the model on the tape while he followed along in his book.

Afterward, Ron read the story orally to Mrs. Yoder. She supported (scaffolded) Ron's attempts to read the story by prompting him to use word analysis strategies when he encountered words that were unknown to him. If Ron did not read a word or read a word incorrectly after sufficient prompts, Mrs. Yoder provided the correct reading of the word. She also printed all the words Ron had read both incorrectly and he had read correctly on flashcards (index cards). While Ron was reading the story, Mrs. Yoder offered frequent verbal praise for words read correctly and for efforts made to read words accurately. After Ron finished reading the story, Mrs. Yoder and Ron played a "Go fish" game that required Ron to read the words on the cards in order to find a match from Mrs. Yoder or from the deck of cards with the words printed on them. Then Mrs. Yoder and Ron played a game of "Hangman" using the words. Once the games were completed, Mrs. Yoder asked a peer to drill Ron on reading the words using the flashcards. Ron was then asked to read the passage again, and the process was repeated until he read the story with 100 percent accuracy on two consecutive trials. Ron charted his accuracy level daily. Once he mastered the story, he was able to choose from a selection of privileges, such as an extra break period.

WHAT CAN SCHOOL PSYCHOLOGISTS AND OTHER EDUCATIONAL CONSULTANTS DO?

1. Observe instruction to determine if effective teaching principles are applied and to what extent they are applied for children who are experiencing challenges.
2. If principles are not applied, help teachers incorporate them, which can be systematically implemented to help children improve their reading performance.
3. If the principles were applied but in a haphazard fashion or at very low rates, help teachers systematically implement the principles or increase their use by closely examining teachers' instruction and by identifying how and when to incorporate the principles.
4. Provide assistance on an individual basis or a systems-level basis (school building or district).

SUMMARY POINTS

- Effective principles of teaching can be applied while using just about every reading technique or program.
- Activating students' prior knowledge can guide their learning and ease their way in reading new content and learning new skills.
- Conducting a task analysis involves ordering reading skills in terms of a step-by-step progression for completing a task.
- *Explicit instruction* means clearly describing the skill that is being taught and teaching it as described.
- *Modeling* is performing an action or exhibiting a behavior for others to imitate; *demonstrating* is describing or explaining an action or behavior when it is being performed.
- Providing students with several opportunities to respond, such as frequent oral storybook reading, promotes active engagement.
- Repeated practice of reading the same word or passage leads to reading mastery.
- Positive reinforcers can be delivered in successive approximations as a way to shape reading accurately and quickly.

- *Scaffolding* reading behaviors mean providing necessary supports and gradually removing those supports as children exhibit reading behavior independently.
- *Generalization* can be promoted by providing children with opportunities to perform the same reading skills in multiple contexts.

QUESTIONS FOR DISCUSSION

1. How may prior knowledge and schemata play a role in students' reading new content? How can educators help students use prior knowledge?
2. Explain the differences between demonstration and modeling of reading skills. Which method is considered a form of explicit instruction?
3. Describe ways in which repeated readings may be used in conjunction with corrective feedback, scaffolding techniques, "teaching to mastery," and generalization of skills.
4. Explain the similarities and differences between using positive reinforcement and providing feedback on students' reading performance.
5. Reread the vignette about Ron and his teacher, Mrs. Yoder. Describe the "effective teaching principles of reading" that Mrs. Yoder used to help Ron with his reading performance.

REFERENCES

Bahrick, H. P., Bahrick, L. E., Bahrick, A. S., & Bahrick, P. E. (1993). Maintenance of foreign language vocabulary and the spacing effect. *Psychological Science, 4*, 316–321.

Barbetta, P. M., Heron, T. E., & Heward, W. L. (1993). Effects of active student responses during error correction on the acquisition, maintenance, and generalization of sight words by students with developmental disabilities. *Journal of Applied Behavior Analysis, 26*, 111–119.

Barbetta, P. M., Heward, W. L., Bradley, D. M., & Miller, A. D. (1994). Effects of immediate and delayed error correction on the acquisition and maintenance of basic sight words by students with developmental disabilities. *Journal of Applied Behavior Analysis, 27*, 177–178.

Baumann, J. F. (1984). The effectiveness of a direct instruction paradigm for teaching main idea comprehension. *Reading Research Quarterly, 20*, 93–115.

Carnine, D. W., Silbert, J., Kame'enui, E. J., & Tarver, S. G. (Eds.). (2004). *Direct Reading Instruction.* (4th ed.). Upper Saddle River, NJ: Pearson.

Daly, E. J., III, Chafouleas, S., & Skinner, C. H. (2005). *Interventions for Reading Problems: Designing and Evaluating Effective Strategies.* New York: Guilford Press.

Daly, E. J., III, & Martens, B. K. (1994). A comparison of three interventions for increasing oral reading performance: Application of the instructional hierarchy. *Journal of Applied Behavior Analysis, 27,* 459–469.

Englemann, S., & Bruner, E. (1988). *Reading Mastery I: DISTAR Reading.* Chicago: Science Research Associates.

Fredrick, L. D., & Hummel, J. H. (2004). Reviewing the outcomes and principles of effective instruction. In D. J. Moran & R. W. Malott (Eds.), *Evidence-Based Educational Methods* (pp. 9–21). San Diego, CA: Elsevier Academic Press.

Gambrell, L. B., & Massoni, S. A. (1999). Principles of best practice: Finding the common ground. In L. B. Gambrell, L. M. Morrow, S. B. Neuman, & M. Pressley (Eds.), *Best Practices in Literacy Instruction* (pp. 11–21). New York: Guilford Press.

Gettinger, M., & Siebert, J. (2002). Increasing academic learning time. In A. Thomas & J. Grimes (Eds.), *Best Practices in School Psychology IV* (pp. 773–788). Bethesda, MD: National Association of School Psychologists.

Hale, A. D., Skinner, C. H., Winn, B. D., Oliver, R., Allin, J. D., & Molloy, C. (2005). An investigation of listening and listening while reading accommodations on comprehension levels and rates in students with emotional disorders. *Psychology in the Schools, 42,* 39–51.

Hummel, J. H., Venn, M. L., & Gunter, P. L. (2004). Teacher-made scripted lessons. In D. J. Moran & R. W. Malott (Eds.), *Evidence-Based Educational Methods* (pp. 9–21). San Diego, CA: Elsevier Academic Press.

McCormick, S. (Ed.). (2003). *Instructing Students Who Have Literacy Problems.* Upper Saddle River, NJ: Prentice Hall.

McCurdy, B. L., Cundari, L., & Lentz, F. E. (1990). Enhancing instructional efficiency: An examination of time delay and the opportunity to observe instruction. *Education and Treatment of Children, 13,* 226–238.

National Reading Panel. (2000). *Teaching Children to Read: An Evidence-Based Assessment of the Scientific Research Literature on Reading and Its Implications for Reading Instruction.* Washington, D.C.: NICHD. Retrieved July 26, 2005 from www.nichd.nih.gov/publications/nrp/smallbook.htm

Orelove, F. P. (1982). Acquisition of incidental learning in moderately and severely handicapped adults. *Education and Training of the Mentally Retarded, 17,* 131–136.

Pany, D., & McCoy, K. M. (1998). Effects of corrective feedback on word accuracy and reading comprehension of readers with learning disabilities. *Journal of Learning Disabilities, 21,* 546–550.

Pressley, M. (1999). Self-regulated comprehension processing and its development through instruction. In L. B. Gambrell, L. M. Morrow, S. B. Neuman, & M. Pressley (Eds.), *Best Practices in Literacy Instruction* (pp. 90–97). New York: Guilford Press.

Rasinski, T. (1990). Effects of repeated reading and listening while reading on reading fluency. *Journal of Educational Research, 83,* 147–150.

Rasinski, T. V., & Hoffman, J. V. (2003). Oral reading in the school literacy curriculum. *Reading Research Quarterly, 38,* 510–522.

Rosenshine, B. (1995). Advances in research in instruction. *Journal of Educational Research, 88,* 262–268.

Skinner, B. F. (1958). Reinforcement today. *American Psychologist, 13,* 94–99.

Skinner, C. H., Cooper, L., & Cole, C. L. (1997). The effects of oral presentation rates on student reading performance. *Journal of Applied Behavior Analysis, 30,* 331–333.

Skinner, C. H., Logan, P., Robinson, D. H., & Robinson, S. L. (1997). Myths and realities of modeling as a reading intervention: Beyond acquisition. *School Psychology Review, 26,* 437–447.

Skinner, C. H, Pappas, D. N., & Davis, K. A. (2005). Enhancing academic engagement: Providing opportunities for responding and influencing students to choose to respond. *Psychology in the Schools, 42,* 389–403.

Slocum, T. A. (2004). Direct instruction: The big ideas. In D. J. Moran & R. W. Malott (Eds.), *Evidence-Based Educational Methods* (pp. 81–91). San Diego, CA: Elsevier Academic Press.

Swanson, H. L. (2001). Research on intervention for adolescents with learning disabilities: A meta-analysis of outcomes related to higher-order processing. *Elementary School Journal, 101,* 331–348.

Swanson, H. L., & Hoskyn, M. (1998). Experimental intervention research on students with learning disabilities: A meta-analysis of treatment outcomes. *Review of Educational Research, 68,* 277–321.

Vaughn, S., Gersten, R., & Chard, D. J. (2000). The underlying message in LD intervention research: Findings from research syntheses. *Exceptional Children, 67,* 99–114.

Chapter 5

Word-Level Interventions

Mr. Jones, a school psychologist, recalls a special-education teacher with 30 years of experience who suggested teaching children with learning disabilities to walk on a balance beam to help them improve their reading skills. Mr. Jones replied, "Yikes, show me the evidence that this works!"

Mr. Jones is not alone in his response to a professional who is unaware of scientifically based intervention practices. For many decades and across various educational settings, well-intentioned professionals have used instructional methods that have not been supported by empirical research. However, school psychologists and educational consultants have an ethical obligation to promote scientifically based reading practices for school-age pupils (National Association of School Psychologists, 2000). Intervention ideas obtained from workshops, faculty meetings, books, newsletters, and even peer-reviewed journals are not necessarily those that have been proven effective through rigorous scholarly investigations. So what constitute evidence-based interventions?

OVERVIEW OF EVIDENCE-BASED INTERVENTIONS

In 1999, a Task Force on Evidence-Based Interventions in School Psychology was established and supported by the Division of School Psychology of the American Psychological Association and the Society for the Study of School Psychology. The task force was formed to support practitioners and researchers as they select, design, and implement intervention techniques, strategies, and programs across all domains of practice. The definition of the term *evidence-based interventions* is evolving (Stoiber & Kratochwill, 2001). Although the task of identifying evidence-based interventions was more complex than the task force had anticipated, the members felt that it was important for school psychology practitioners and researchers to have some guidelines for selecting scientifically supported interventions (Kratochwill & Stoiber, 2002). The task force described evidence-based interventions as those that have a theoretical foundation, are valid, have been tested using sound research methodologies, and are appropriate for the setting in which they are intended to be used (Stoiber & Kratochwill, 2001).

The task force developed the *Procedural and Coding Manual for Identification of Evidence-Based Interventions* to facilitate the use of criteria and a coding structure for evaluating studies reporting on the effects of interventions (Kratochwill & Stoiber, 2002). Users of this manual, which is available at the task force's website (www.sp-ebi.org), can code and evaluate interventions on the following criteria: whether they were described procedurally and precisely so they could be replicated with ease, whether they used controlled comparison groups (randomized for between-group studies) and conditions with experimental controls (particularly for within-group studies), whether they used valid and reliable multi-outcome data-based measures, whether they used procedural integrity methods, and whether there was evidence of durable and generalized effects (Stoiber & Kratochwill, 2001). Other considerations that are particularly relevant to applied settings such as schools include whether the benefits of the interventions outweigh the costs, whether the interventions can be implemented from an instructional time perspective, whether extensive training and resources are needed, and other social validity factors (Kratochwill & Stoiber, 2002). Examples of coding of various types of research studies (i.e., single-subject and group-based design) have been described in the literature (Lewis-Snyder, Stoiber, & Kratochwill, 2002; Shernoff, Kratochwill, & Stoiber, 2002).

The criteria and guidelines for identifying evidence-based interventions are consistent with the scientifically based components outlined in the No Child Left Behind Act of 2001 (U.S. Department of Education). The legislation places a heavy emphasis on identifying educational practices that have proved, through rigorous experimental analysis, to produce positive academic achievement outcomes for students and those practices that fit into a curriculum for a given school setting. This mandate has prompted statewide educational agencies, particularly school districts, to account for the educational practices they use to facilitate academic achievement goals. Many school districts throughout the United States struggle with meeting performance-based standards as measured on statewide tests. This is especially the case for schools serving populations of children living in poverty.

The good news is that using scientifically based intervention practices will likely increase the chances that they will be effective in meeting individual students' needs (Brown-Chidsey & Steege, 2005; Moran, 2004). Many educators ask, "How do we locate evidence-based reading practices?" The easy answer is to consult the high-quality scholarly journals (e.g., *Journal of Applied Behavior Analysis, Journal of Educational Psychology, Journal of Special Education, Learning Disability Quarterly, Reading Research Quarterly, School Psychology Review*) for articles that report research on reading instruction. However, becoming familiar with high-quality journals is the beginning and not the end of the process. The next step is to become a critical consumer of research. This is not easy for educational professionals who do not have sufficient training and experience in identifying strengths and limitations of investigations. Unfortunately, even some professionals who have obtained graduate degrees are not necessarily good consumers of research. In order to meet national, state, and local policies requiring the implementation of evidence-based instructional practices in the schools, every professional working in schools, regardless of specific role or degree, should receive training on how to be critical consumers of research *and* how to test whether the interventions are effective in meeting their own students' needs in the classroom. Emphasis on this area of professional competency also should be infused across the curriculum for all preservice educational training programs nationwide. This applies to all prospective educational professionals, regardless of the position they plan to hold (speech and language therapist, school psychologist, principal, teacher) or what grade level or content area they are preparing to teach. (Chapter 7 presents methods that practitioners and researchers can use for evaluating the effectiveness of interventions on individual students.)

A good deal of research has been done in the field of reading instruction; however, much more needs to be done before conclusions can be made on what constitutes effective instruction for all reading skill areas and age groups. The most extensive and robust studies have been in the area of phonological awareness and word reading instruction for primary-grade students. Far fewer studies have addressed the effects of basic reading skills instruction for adolescent populations. Likewise, data from existing research are inconclusive as to the most effective methods to teach children of all ages reading comprehension skills (National Reading Panel, 2000). We are bound to see a significant increase in studies along these lines as researchers respond to the continued emphasis on reading in the high stakes assessment of student and school achievement and the increasing focus on high school outcomes. The evolution of research in reading instruction makes it imperative that educational consultants stay informed on current research so that they can help educators replace ineffective and unsupported reading instruction with evidence-based, supported methods.

VARIOUS TYPES OF WORD-LEVEL INTERVENTIONS

Word-level interventions are those designed to help students read words accurately in and out of connected text. Students should be provided with as many opportunities as possible to acquire words in the context of connected text. However, in some instances words need to be taught in isolation so that children can examine features of particular words without the distraction of other words and punctuation marks in connected text (McCormick, 2003). The following provides a description of various strategies, techniques, and programs for developing phonological awareness, phonic analysis, whole (sight) word recognition, and word reading fluency. Phonic and whole word instruction methods are critical to helping students become proficient readers, and both should be part of the curricula and practices for comprehensive literacy instruction. These interventions can be adapted to working with individuals or small or large groups of children. They can be used in a general education program, special education program, special reading programs, and speech and language programs. These strategies, techniques, and programs can be used in conjunction with each other or with others not mentioned in this book. Some of the strategies, techniques, and programs described here have been tested through rigorous scientific research, and some need further investigation but hold promise for being valid techniques that will likely help students achieve word reading skills. A description of each strategy, technique, or program will include its purpose, the materials or resources needed, the procedures, and the evidence supporting its use.

Phonological Awareness

As mentioned in chapter 1, children who have phonological awareness skills are likely to develop word reading skills with more ease. There are a variety of evidence-supported phonological awareness instruction activities. The instruction techniques described here are designed to teach a multitude of phonological awareness skills, such as phoneme blending, segmentation, isolation, categorization, and others.

Sound Manipulation Activities

Yopp and Yopp (2000) advocate the use of a variety of sound manipulation activities for helping children develop phoneme awareness. In the following sound manipulation activities, the teacher delivers explicit instructions. These activities can be modified to be more gamelike by using pictures, boards (such as bingo boards), tiles, jingles, and other materials. Sound matching involves detecting whether sounds in two or more words are the same. Materials for this activity may include pictures of objects, though they are not necessary for completing the activity.

Isolating sounds in words involves identifying beginning, middle, and ending sounds in isolation. The teacher may say the words *hat* and *horn* and ask the children if the words begin with the same sound. Or the teacher may say, "What do you hear at the beginning of the word *fan?*" Children are asked to respond by making the /f/ sound. The same technique can be used when teaching ending sounds as well.

Substituting sounds in words involves replacing one sound with another to form a different word, such as replacing the /d/ sound in *dime* with an /l/ sound to make *lime*.

Sound deletion involves removing a sound and saying the remaining word without the sound in it, such as removing the sound /tr/ in the word *treat* and leaving the remaining word *eat*. Sound addition may involve saying the word *rain* and adding the /st/ sound to make the word *strain*.

Sound blending is one of the easiest phoneme awareness activities (Yopp, 1988). Blending activities can progress from blending the initial sound onto the rest of the word, blending syllables of a word together, and then blending isolated phonemes into a word

(Edelen-Smith, 1997). The teacher might model these tasks by saying "It starts with /c/ and ends with /at/, and when it is put together, it is *cat*." The teacher then might say, "It starts with /c/ and it ends with /ake/, and when it is put together, it makes what word?" The children are instructed to supply the word. In this activity, children are also encouraged to lead the activity with the other children by coming up with sounds of words to blend together. Teaching a more advanced blending skill may involve the teacher segmenting sounds of a word such as s-u-n, and the children respond by saying the blended word.

Sound segmentation involves the teacher saying a word and asking the children to say the individual sounds of the word, such as saying p-a-n for the word *pan*. Sound manipulation activities have been related to reading development in young children (Wagner, Torgesen, Laughon, Simmons, & Raschotte, 1993).

Sound Boxes

This technique was first described by D. B. Elkonin (1973) and has been called Elkonin boxes. The technique is designed to help children segment sounds of spoken words in a sequential fashion (phoneme segmentation) as well as make them aware of the positions of sounds in spoken words (i.e., beginning, middle, and ending, in positional analysis). Materials that are needed to implement this technique may include pictures depicting an object (this is particularly the case for young children and older children with severe phonological deficits), a rectangle divided into sections that form connected boxes, and tokens or other small objects that can easily slide onto the boxes. The connected boxes can be drawn on a magnetic board or dry-erase board or can be laminated on cardboard for most appealing use for young children. However, the connected boxes can also be placed on a worksheet. The tokens can be magnets, game board chips or checkers, or coins. Figure 5-1 provides a visual depiction of this technique.

The instructor begins the task by placing a picture of an object above the connected boxes (drawn on a dry-erase board that is lying flat on a table or desk) and then placing the tokens below the connected boxes. The number of linked boxes drawn and the number of tokens correspond to the number of sounds heard in a word. For instance, three connected boxes and three tokens would be used for the word *cat*. The instructor articulates the word slowly and demonstrates by sliding the tokens into the connected boxes as each sound of the word is pronounced. For example, after placing a picture of a cat above the divided rectangle, the instructor slowly articulates the word *cat* and slides the first token in the first connected box while saying /c/, then slides the second token into the second box while saying /a/, and so forth. After modeling the task for the children, the instructor then shares the task with the children by having them articulate the word slowly while she slides the tokens into the connected boxes. The instructor gives the children a set of materials and they can complete the process by articulating the word slowly and simultaneously sliding the tokens into their own respective boxes. The instructor provides feedback on children's responses and corrects mistakes or models the process again. For the remainder of words presented, the instructor can state, "Now, say it and move it."

Figure 5-1. *Use of sound boxes for segmenting the word "Cat."*

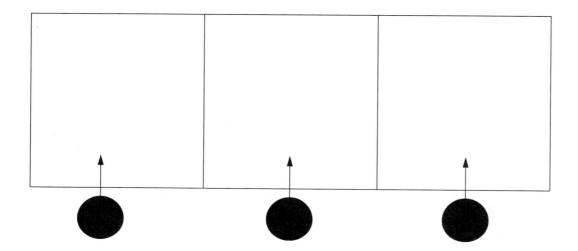

During the positional analysis phase of the activity, tokens are gathered and placed to the side of the connected boxes. The instructor may ask the children to place a token in the box where they hear a certain sound in a word. For instance, the instructor may ask, "Where do you hear the /a/ sound in the word *cat?*" Children then place their token in the middle box. They place a token in the first box when the teacher asks, "Where do you hear the /c/ sound in the word?" and so forth. This process is designed to help children become aware of beginning, middle, and ending sounds. Through his observations, D. B. Elkonin found that this process helped children become aware of discrete sounds and the sounds' positions in a word, and helped them develop the sequential skills needed to blend the sounds to form a whole word. Elkonin's boxes have been modified slightly and are commonly referred to as the *say it– move it* activity. This technique works well with all types of word patterns, such as consonant-vowel (CV), consonant-vowel-consonant (CVC), consonant-vowel-consonant-silent vowel (CVCV), consonant-vowel-vowel-consonant (CVVC), and consonant-consonant-vowel-consonant (CCVC), as well as with words with more complex sound patterns (multisyllabic words).

Landmark studies that demonstrate the effectiveness of phonemic awareness training with young children have included the use of sound boxes (the *say it–move it* activity; Ball & Blachman, 1991; Bentin & Leshem, 1993; Bryne & Fielding-Barnsley, 1991; Hohn &

Ehri, 1983). Other studies have supported the use of this technique especially for helping preschoolers segment sounds and isolate middle sounds in words (Maslanka & Joseph, 2002). This technique and several variations of sound boxes (sometimes referred to as *say it-move it* activities) have been described in Blachman, Ball, Black, and Tangel's (2000) book, *Road to the Code: A Phonological Awareness Program for Young Children*. This resource contains forty-four lessons aimed to teach a multitude of sounds and sound patterns.

Sound Sorts

Sound sorts are activities that have been extensively described and illustrated in Bear, Invernizzi, Templeton, & Johnston's (1996) book, *Words Their Way: Word Study for Phonics, Vocabulary, and Spelling*. This technique is designed to help children detect spoken words that share similar sounds and those that sound different. *Sound sorts* involve categorizing, for instance, common beginning, middle, and ending sounds of words. Materials include cutout pictures in sizes that are manageable for sorting. Bear et al. contains pages filled with pictures to be cut out to give teachers a start at developing the materials for this activity. The instructor establishes categories of sounds by placing pictures representing things that begin with different letter sounds; for instance, for things that begin with the /b/ sound, the category picture is a picture of a ball.

Initially, the instructor may wish to demonstrate the procedures for students. While pointing to the pictures, the instructor says the names of the pictures, emphasizing the beginning sound of the word. He or she then gives a student a stack of picture cards and asks the student to orally name the picture and sort it by placing it beneath the category picture card that begins with the same sound. More picture card categories can be established as the students become familiar with the task. Once all the picture cards have been sorted, the students can read the words and be encouraged to self-monitor their sorts and to make corrections if a picture was sorted in the wrong place. Prompting and feedback can be given on students' responses.

Sound categorization activities have been used in investigations. For instance, Maslanka and Joseph's (2002) preliminary study compared groups of preschoolers' performance in sound sort and sound box interventions, using a number of phonological processing variables. Their results indicated that both groups made gains in performance from pretest to posttest periods. Methods involving categorizing sounds have been related to learning to read for young children (Bradley & Bryant, 1983). Figure 5-2 presents an illustration of a sound sort task.

Phonic Analysis Techniques

Phonics instruction focuses on teaching letter-sound correspondences. Stahl (1992) offered some key components of exemplary phonics instruction. They include (a) building on children's concepts about the functions of print or what reading is all about, (b) building on phonemic awareness skills, (c) delivering instruction in a direct or explicit manner, (d) integrating phonics into a comprehensive reading program, (e) emphasizing reading words rather

Figure 5-2. *Sorting sounds according to initial sound of objects.*

SOUND SORT

than learning rules, (f) teaching onset and rimes, (g) focusing on strategies for decoding words, (h) focusing on internal structures of words, and (i) developing automaticity in recognizing words so that attention can be devoted to comprehending text. With regard to rules, Stahl realized that fewer than half of the rules apply to the majority of words and so are best taught as a way of pointing out certain spelling patterns, such as vowel patterns in words. The following interventions, strategies, and programs are designed to teach phonic analysis skills.

Onsets and Rimes

Onsets refer to the part of the syllable before the vowel, and rimes refer to the part of the syllable from the vowel onward. The purpose of teaching phonics using onsets and rimes is to help children acquire the letter-sound correspondences that are found among particular spelling patterns or in sequences (strings) of letters within words. A string of letters in a particular sequence will typically make the same sound across many words. For example, the rime /ack/ shares a similar sound in words such as *back, lack, sack, knack, crack,* and *stack.* These words are also often called *word family* words or phonograms. Children can learn to read many words easily in a relatively short time because of the *generative* units these words possess (Johnston, 1999). Adams (1990) reported that there are approximately 286 phonograms that appear commonly in primary-grade texts, and 95 percent of them are pronounced the same in every word in which they appear. Nearly five hundred words can be derived from the following thirty-seven rimes:

-ack	-ain	-ake	-ale	-all	-ame
-an	-ank	-ap	-ash	-at	-ate
-aw	-ay	-eat	-ell	-est	-ice
-ick	-ide	-ight	-ill	-in	-ine
-ing	-ink	-ip	-ir	-ock	-oke
-op	-or	-ore	-uck	-up	-ump
-unk					

Materials can include a multitude of objects that students can manipulate, such as plastic, tile, or magnetic letters; a magnetic board; and words printed on a cardboard strip with a slit where onsets slide in and out. Computer programs can also be designed to make onsets and rimes. An example of a procedure may be placing the rimes on a magnetic board and having the student substitute various onsets to make "new" words that sound similar. The students are instructed to read the words once they are created. These words can then be used to create a word wall (see Wagstaff, 1997, and Cunningham, 1995, for instructions and illustrations). Onsets and rimes are useful for teaching words by analogy, a method that has been effective on basic reading skill performance (Gaskins et al., 1988; Goswami, 1986). For example, once children are taught to read the word *cat,* they can easily learn to read the words *bat, sat,* and *hat.*

Word Boxes

Word boxes, an extension of sound boxes and a modification of Clay's (1993) letter boxes, are used as a part of reading recovery lessons when children have trouble making

Figure 5-3. *Using word boxes to make letter-sound correspondences for the word "Cat."*

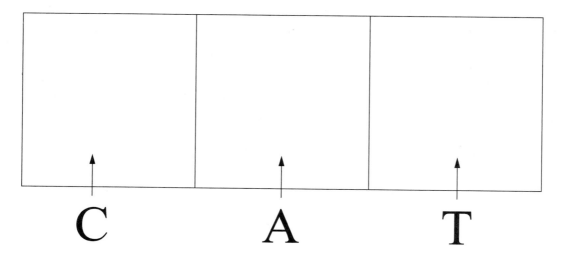

one-to-one sequential correspondences between letters and sounds in words. The word boxes technique is designed to help students make sequential letter-sound associations (see Figure 5-3). The materials needed for this technique are the same as those used for sound boxes, except the tokens are replaced with plastic or tile lowercase letters. The children are asked to slide letters in the connected boxes as they slowly articulate the sounds of a word. Where letter patterns make one sound, the children slide all the letters that make that particular sound into one of the connected boxes. For example, the word *boat* contains two letters in the middle of the word that make one vowel sound. Therefore, three connected boxes are displayed, and the children slide the "o" and the "a" into the middle box as they say the /oa/ sound. The letter "b" is placed in the first box and the letter "t" is placed in the last box as they say these sounds.

Another phase of the word boxes technique may require children to write the letters in the appropriate boxes as they slowly articulate the sounds. This practice may also help develop spelling skills. As the children learn to perform the task, the lines that divide the rectangle into boxes can be drawn as dotted lines and then can be erased, leaving a rectangle without the divided sections (i.e., gradually fading the structure). Eventually, the separate sound boxes and then the rectangle can be taken away, and the children can perform the task without the supportive structure (scaffolding). Demonstration and corrective feedback may be given, depending on the children's responses.

Although more research needs to be done to establish the efficacy of this technique, word boxes have shown some promise in helping children improve their word recognition and spelling performance (Joseph, 1998/1999; 2000a; 2000b; 2002). Word boxes can be used to teach students to decode words that they find difficult to read in connected text (Clay, 1993).

Word Sorts

Similar to sound sorts, word sorts are considered to be a spelling-based phonic word study technique for distinguishing spelling patterns among words (Bear et al., 1996). Materials include index cards with words printed on them. The instructor establishes the category words by placing two or more index cards with words printed on them in front of the child. She says the category words and gives the child a stack of index cards with words printed on them to sort and place below the appropriate category words. After the child has completed the sort, the instructor asks the child to read the words aloud, encouraging the child to self-monitor his or her responses by correcting mistakes, such as a word that has been sorted into the wrong category. Children can catalog their sorts in a portfolio and refer back to it to help them pronounce or spell a word. The instructor may need to demonstrate the sorting procedures before children are able to complete them more independently.

Words can be sorted according to several features, including common spelling, sound, or morphemic features (Zutell, 1998). Sorting according to word families or phonograms (e.g., cat, hat, bat, sat, set, pet, net, bet, sit, fit, kit, bit) is frequently used with primary-grade children (Figure 5-4 illustrates a word sort technique with onsets and rimes). An example of a morphemic or meaning-based sort would involve words ending in "ian" (e.g., pediatrician, magician, musician) below the category "people," and sorting words ending in "ion" (e.g., institution, education, constitution) below the category "things."

The effectiveness of word sorts has been explored in a few investigations. Joseph (2000a) explored their effects on phonemic awareness, word recognition, and spelling and found that they affected spelling performance. Other studies also reported on their effectiveness for helping children with mental retardation improve their basic reading and spelling performance (Joseph, 2002, Joseph & McCachran, 2003). A particularly interesting finding revealed that combining word sorts and the "copy cover check" procedure produced better spelling performance for children than either of the techniques alone (Dangel, 1989). Positive outcomes have also been demonstrated in studies that included word sorts as part of a comprehensive reading program, such as Early Steps, for teaching disadvantaged pupils (Santa & Hoien, 1999) and Howard Street Tutoring Program (Morris, Shaw, & Perney, 1990), as well as other phonics-based classroom instruction programs (Juel & Midden-Cup, 2000). Word sorts are also used within the Four Blocks program (Cunningham, 1999).

Figure 5-4. *Sorting words according to similar sound and spelling patterns.*

WORD SORT

Cat	Cut	Cot
Bat	Rut	Dot
Sat	Gut	Pot
Mat	Hut	Not
Pat	Nut	Hot
Fat	But	Got

More research needs to be conducted before conclusions can be drawn validating this approach to teaching reading and spelling. The studies mentioned here as well as others (e.g., Joseph & Orlins, 2005) seem to provide preliminary support for the multiple uses of this technique, especially for studying about the phonic, spelling, and morphemic patterns of words.

Whole (Sight) Word Techniques

Children need to be able to eventually learn to read words by sight or as a whole, which means reading words automatically or effortlessly rather than reading slowly and pausing in between letter sounds. Learning to read words effortlessly leads to fluency, which leads to better comprehension of text. Several techniques are available for teaching children to read words as a whole.

Traditional Flashcard Drill and Practice

This technique uses a flashcard drill to teach children to rapidly read words that are unknown to them. The instructor models the drill by presenting a flashcard with a word printed on it, reading the word, asking the student to read the word, and then providing the student with feedback. The teacher then presents the flashcards one after the other and asks the student to read the words. The flashcards are shuffled between drills, and feedback is given to the student after he or she reads the word. This method and slight variations of this procedure are commonly used by educators and have been found to be effective for increasing word recognition skills and comprehension (Tan & Nicholson, 1997). In comparison with other word recognition procedures, this drill has been found to be a time-efficient way to help children learn to read words they don't know (Joseph & Nist, 2006; Schmidgall & Joseph, in press). Traditional drill methods of teaching spelling have also been found to be an efficient way of helping children spell words (Cates et al., 2003).

Interspersal of Known and Unknown Words

The purpose of teaching unknown words with known words is based on reinforcement principles. When children experience success with reading words accurately, their reading behaviors are likely to increase, and they are likely to attempt to read material that is unfamiliar to them (Skinner, 2002). In other words, children are likely to become more actively engaged in reading tasks if they experience success.

Interspersal procedures consist of flashcards with known and unknown words. Known words are interspersed with unknown words at varying ratios. Some researchers advocate a ratio of 50 percent known to 50 percent unknown words; others have advocated less challenging ratios of 90 percent known to 10 percent unknown (Burns, 2004). Determining which ratio to use depends on individual student behaviors and characteristics. For instance, three different known words can be interspersed after three different unknown words. The instructor may present ratios of unknown to known words on flashcards modeling the reading of unknown words when they are initially presented and providing corrective feedback throughout the drill. Several studies have reported the effectiveness of interspersal procedures on reading behaviors (Neef, Iwata, & Page, 1977, 1980; Roberts & Shapiro, 1996; Roberts, Turco, & Shapiro, 1991).

Incremental Rehearsal

Incremental rehearsal is a drill technique that incorporates opportunities to practice learning the content by interspersing 10 percent unknown or new content with 90 percent known or mastered content (Tucker, 1988). The incremental rehearsal technique is different from other interspersal techniques because it incorporates the repeated practice of content incrementally. This technique can be used to teach sight word reading. Materials include index cards.

The process begins by identifying ten words unknown to the student, then printing nine known words and one unknown word on index cards. The instructor presents and reads the first unknown word to the student, uses it in a sentence, and then reads it again. The student is then asked to read the new word. Following the presentation of the first unknown word, the first known word is presented and the student is asked to read it. Then the instructor presents the first unknown word again and asks the student to read it. That is followed by the first known word again and then the second known word. Again the instructor presents the first unknown word for the student to read, followed by the presentation and reading of the first, second, and third known words. This procedure continues until the unknown word has been interspersed incrementally nine times. When this has occurred, the ninth known word is removed from the stack of words and the first unknown word becomes the first known word and thus remains in the stack. A new unknown word is introduced and practiced and this process continues until the ten unknown words become known words. MacQuarrie, Tucker, Burns, and Hartman (2002) found this technique helped children to retain reading words better than other types of interspersal techniques or a traditional drill technique. Incremental rehearsal can also help build fluency and comprehension (Burns, Dean, & Foley, 2004). This incremental rehearsal procedure is similar to "folding in" flash card drill procedures, in which unknown words are folded in with the known words (Shapiro, 2004).

Repeated Readings

The purpose of repeated readings is to increase oral reading fluency, that is, reading words in passages accurately, quickly, and with expression (Samuels, 1979). Materials include a stopwatch and appropriate grade-level reading materials. It is recommended that students be provided with short passages that contain fifty to three hundred words, with 85 percent of the words read correctly in the initial reading (criterion levels of fluency). Students are given one minute to read the passage. The instructor has a copy of the passage so that he or she can record the number of words read accurately and the miscues. The student is asked to read the passage a second time, again for one minute, to determine how many more words the student can read accurately. The readings are repeated until the student reads the passage accurately at an acceptable rate. Once the criterion levels of fluency have been achieved, a more difficult text is introduced and the procedure is repeated.

Research has clearly documented the effects of repeated readings on improving reading fluency of pupils at many grade levels (Carver, 1997; Downhower, 1987; Herman, 1985; Mercer, Campbell, Miller, Mercer, & Lane, 2000; O'Shea, Sindelar, & O'Shea, 1985; Weinstein & Cooke, 1992). A review of various oral reading instruction methods revealed that repeated readings were the most effective technique for building fluency (Kuhn &

Stahl, 2003). The use of repeated readings for building fluency has also been found to improve the comprehension performance of students with and without disabilities (see Therrien, 2004, for a review of studies). Repeated readings are often used in conjunction with other reading instruction methods. For instance, corrective feedback methods can be used in response to miscues during repeated readings (e.g., Nelson, Alber, & Grody, 2004).

Phrase Drill With Repeated Reading

The phrase drill is one type of corrective feedback procedure that can be used during repeated readings of passages. The purpose of this feedback technique is to give students corrective feedback on miscues and provide opportunities to practice reading miscued words accurately in the context of connected text (Daly, Chafouleas, & Skinner, 2005). Materials include two copies of reading passages (for the student and the instructor) and a highlighter marker. The student reads a passage orally for one minute, and the instructor follows along and highlights or underlines the errors the student is making. After the student finishes reading the passage, the instructor shows the student the highlighted copy. The instructor models the correct reading of the error word to the student. The student is then asked to read each error word aloud three times. If more than one error word occurs in a sentence, the instructor models the correct reading of all error words before having the student read the sentence three times. This procedure promotes generalization of the correct reading of the words in connected text (Daly, Lentz, & Boyer, 1996; Daly & Martens, 1994).

Listening While Reading

The purpose of this method is to model accurate oral reading. This is used especially for students who read many words inaccurately and read at a very slow rate (Daly, Chafouleas, & Skinner, 2005). Materials include reading passages and may consist of a tape recorder. The instructor gives the reading passage to the student and tells the student to follow along with his or her finger to learn how to read the words as the instructor reads the passage. The instructor reads at an appropriate rate and checks to see if the student can easily follow along. The passage can be prerecorded and played on a tape recorder and the instructor can guide the student in following along with the reading. After reading the whole passage, the instructor asks the student to read the passage aloud.

Listening while reading is different from listening to tape recordings of passages in learning centers, because children are observed sweeping their fingers across the page and are asked to read the same passage aloud after listening to the passage being read to them (Johns & Berglund, 2002). This procedure has been found to be effective for helping children read text more accurately and quickly (Daly & Martens, 1994; Skinner et al., 1993) and helping them comprehend text at higher rates than a silent reading control condition (Hale, Skinner, Winn, Oliver, Allin, & Molloy, 2005). This modeling procedure has also been used effectively in conjunction with repeated reading exercises (Rasinski, 1990).

Paired Reading

The purpose of paired reading is to improve children's oral reading fluency (Topping, 1995). In paired reading, a more skilled reader is paired with a less skilled reader. Both read the same text aloud alongside each other. The more fluent reader adjusts his reading rate to make it comfortable for the less fluent reader to follow and read along. The less fluent reader may read parts of the text independently, and the more fluent reader joins in again when the less fluent reader has difficulty decoding the text. As soon as errors occur during paired reading, they are corrected by the more skilled reader. Research has yielded promising results of this method for helping less skilled readers read accurately and comprehend text better (Topping, 1987; Knapp and Winsor, 1998).

Readers' Theater

This technique can be used to build fluency. On occasion, it can be used as a diversion from repeated reading exercises. Readers' theater actually incorporates repeated reading of scripts (Rasinski, 2000). Materials include stories and scripts that are based on those stories. The instructor selects a script and then reads aloud from the story that the script is based on to model fluent reading with expression. The instructor teaches students to pay attention to signals in the text that might help them know how the characters are feeling so that the students have a sense of how the characters might sound. Students are given scripts to read aloud with each other and at home for practice. The next school day, they are asked to practice reading the scripts aloud again to select students to read certain roles. Students are asked to reread their roles. Eventually, the students perform the production in front of an audience. Readers' theater has yielded positive results as an oral reading method for young children (Keehn, 2003).

Multiple Exposure/Multiple Context

The purpose of this approach is to teach children to acquire reading words in and out of connected text by providing several opportunities to learn and practice reading words in many contexts or using multiple techniques (McCormick, 2003). The approach is used particularly for severely delayed or nonreaders, although many of the components can be used to teach a multitude of phonic and sight word reading skills to all types of readers. Materials include a high-interest book series that progresses in difficulty from book to book, and a game such as bingo, hangman, or "go fish." Chapter books are good sources to use for this activity, with the easiest book written at a simple preprimer level. In chapter books, each book is divided into approximately five chapters that tell a single story. The majority of the vocabulary in these books is controlled so that the same words (no more than ten in most cases) are used repeatedly throughout the chapters.

In this technique, the student is asked to read the story unassisted to establish a baseline level of all the words known and unknown to the reader. The instructor makes a note of all the words the student cannot read and records the words on index cards. The book is then set aside and the student learns to read the words through a variety of word reading techniques. The various word reading techniques described in this section, such as word boxes, word sorts, and interspersal techniques, can be used to teach the unknown words. Students can practice reading words they don't know by using cutout words that can be put together to form sentences. Sentences written on strips of paper can be used with a box drawn around the unknown word. The teacher can read all the words in the sentence and ask the student to read the unknown word or read the word in the box.

Word reading games can be used to motivate the student and provide a less intimidating, interesting way of using the word multiple times and in different contexts. A bingo game can be used to help children recognize the unknown word when it is called out. Matching games or "go fish" can be played between instructor and student as a way to recognize the unknown words. Or guessing word games such as "hangman" can be played. As students master reading the unknown words, the words are placed in a word bank, which could mean placing the index cards with the mastered words on a ring. From session to session, the student can see how the bank or the collection of index cards on a ring is growing. Charts and game boards can also be used to keep score of how many words the student is acquiring. After three to five sessions of practicing the words, the student is asked to read the chapter again. His or her performance is recorded and the process is repeated until all the words in the chapter can be read effortlessly (mastered). Once this criterion has been reached, the student is asked to read the next chapter, and the process is repeated. McCormick (1994) found that this technique was effective for helping a nonreader become a reader.

READING PROGRAMS AND OTHER RESOURCES

The following section gives an overview of some of the various reading programs and other interventions that have been supported by research, although more research is needed to fully substantiate their use with diverse learners in various contexts.

Reading Programs

The following reading programs incorporate many of the effective principles of instruction that were discussed in chapter 4. This is not an exhaustive presentation of all the programs that have the potential for helping students become proficient readers.

Reading Mastery

The Direct Instruction System for Teaching and Remediation (DISTAR) program was renamed and revised and is now referred to as the Direct Instruction Reading Mastery program (Englemann & Bruner, 1988). The program involves systematic, fast-paced scripted lessons on teaching sounds in isolation, blending sounds, and reading vocabulary words that have regular decodable spellings. The scripted lessons include choral responding, corrective feedback, scaffolding, shaping, and opportunities to practice until mastery is achieved.

This program incorporates just about all of the effective instruction components discussed in chapter 4. A meta-analysis and comprehensive review of studies examining this program found that it has been effective for teaching reading to general and special education pupils and students in elementary and secondary grades (Adams & Englemann, 1996). For instance, Meyer (1984) found this program to have long-term positive effects on reading achievement for children.

Success for All

Success for All is a comprehensive reading program that is divided into smaller programs consisting of a preschool or early kindergarten program, beginning reading or the Reading Roots program, and Beyond the Basics or the Reading Wings program (Slavin, Madden, Karwett, Dolan, & Wasik, 1992). Success for All is specially designed to meet the needs of students who are at risk of reading failure. The preschool or early kindergarten program involves storytelling, retelling, alphabetic activities, and expressive vocabulary activities. The beginning reading program consists of reading rehearsals; metacognitive strategies; story reading; and sound, letter, and word development exercises. The Beyond the Basics program includes a variety of story reading, direct instruction in comprehending text, independent reading, and listening comprehension.

Success for All incorporates continuous progress monitoring, effective instruction components, one-to-one tutoring, and family support. A review of investigations revealed that minority students who attended urban schools and were in the lowest 25 percent for reading performance had improved reading performance as a result of the Success for All program (Ross, Smith, Slavin, & Madden, 1997). Another investigation reported how the program helped kindergartners and first graders achieve word identification and word attack skills (Ross & Smith, 1994).

Phast Program

Phast stands for phonological and strategy training. Five key strategies are taught and applied in a "game plan" format (Lovett, Lacerenza, & Borden, 2000). The game plan consists of students (with the assistance of an instructor) selecting strategies and developing plans to implement those strategies. Once a strategy has been selected and implemented, the students are instructed to monitor their use of the strategy by assessing their performance. Students are encouraged to choose another strategy if the first one they chose did not produce desirable performance results. The strategies include sounding-out, rhyming, peeling-off, vowel-alert, and "I spy."

The sounding-out strategy involves systematic training in letter-sound correspondences, phonological remediation, sound segmentation, sound blending, and phonologically based word identification. This strategy in the game plan incorporates many of the components and lessons contained in the Direct Instruction Reading Mastery program (formerly DISTAR).

The rhyming strategy focuses on teaching words that share common spelling patterns or word family words (i.e., onsets and rimes). Children are taught that these phonograms are key parts of words and can be used for learning other, more complex, words. Instructors give explicit instruction and practice with students to help them develop their word analogy skills (e.g., recognizing that the word *can* makes a similar sound to the words *man* and *fan*.) The peeling-off strategy is used to teach students prefixes and suffixes. In this strategy, the students peel off (segment) the affixes on words to identify the root word.

The vowel-alert strategy entails students trying different vowel pronunciations with an unknown word until they say the word correctly. Children progress from learning single short and long vowel sounds to learning vowel combinations (diphthongs and diagraphs).

The "I spy" strategy is mainly used to teach compound words. For instance, students may say "I spy a pan in the word *pancake*". The students then place a box around the word *pan*; then they may say I spy a cake and place a box around that word. Lovett, Lacerenza, Borden, et al. (2000) found positive outcomes for word identification, passage comprehension, and nonword reading performance for a sample of children who used the "Phast" strategies (combined phonological and strategy training) in contrast to the performance of children who received only phonological training or only strategy training.

Scott Foresman Early Reading Intervention

Formerly called Project Optimize, the Scott Foresman Early Reading Intervention program is based on a five-year longitudinal investigation conducted by Simmons & Kame'enui (1998). The purpose of the program is to provide early intensive instruction on phonological awareness, letter naming, letter sounds, word reading, spelling, and simple sentence reading. The instructional sessions last about thirty minutes and incorporate direct instruction principles. In the first fifteen minutes of every lesson, phonological awareness and alphabetic understanding are taught. This may include working on phoneme segmentation, blending, and sound discrimination and reading consonant-vowel-consonant words in connected text (sentences). The remaining fifteen-minute segment involves spelling words and reinforcing phonological and alphabetic skills.

Orton-Gillingham Phonics

Conceived by Sam Orton and Anna Gillingham, the Orton-Gillingham Phonics program is one of the oldest programs designed to teach children with reading disabilities and was originally developed to provide an organized set of instructional materials and lessons. The Orton-Gillingham program is now in its eighth edition (Gillingham & Stillman, 1997).

The program teaches phonics through multisensory stimuli that provide children with opportunities to link sound to print. For instance, children learn to say words as they write them and are also encouraged to feel their throat muscles as they articulate a sequence of sounds. Basic decodable words and multisyllabic words are taught. Lessons progress in level of difficulty. Several programs are considered to be offshoots of Orton-Gillingham, including Alphabetic Phonics, Project Read, Singerland, Spalding, and Wilson (Henry, 1998). Some research has supported the use of these programs to help children improve their basic reading skills (Foorman, Francis, Beeler, Winikates, & Fletcher, 1997; Stoner, 1991).

Wilson Reading System

Barbara Wilson, the developer of the Wilson Reading System, was an Orton-Gillingham teacher. Her program was also designed to teach reading skills through multisensory methods. The program consists of phoneme segmentation, alphabetic principle, decoding, spelling, advanced word analysis, vocabulary development, sight words, fluency, and comprehension instruction. The lessons are designed to be taught to children in small groups or one-on-one. It incorporates direct instruction as well as metacognitive strategies (an awareness of how language is structured) for developing reading skills. Some investigations have reported on its effects for helping severely delayed readers of various ages (Banks, Guyer, & Guyer, 1993; Bursuck & Dickson, 1999; Clark & Uhry, 1995).

The Lindamood Phoneme Sequencing Program for Reading, Spelling, and Speech (LIPS)

The third edition of the LIPS program, formerly called Auditory Discrimination in Depth, involves reading and spelling simple words for gaining an awareness of sounds, discovering oral-motor features of sounds, labeling sounds and letters, making letter-sound associations, discriminating consonant pairs, classifying vowels, discriminating vowel sounds, and tracking simple sequences of consonant and vowel sounds (same, different, and number of sounds) (Lindamood & Lindamood, 1998). This program and its earlier versions have been effective for developing phonological awareness and basic reading skills (Kennedy & Blackman, 1993; McGuinness, McGuinness, & Donohue, 1995; Torgesen, 2001; Wise, Ring, & Olson, 1999).

Other Resources for Reading Interventions

A number of reading intervention resources can be found on the Internet. Readers are encouraged to follow up on the interventions suggested here by visiting the following websites and conducting a literature search for empirical evidence supporting these methods.

- Intervention Central (www.interventioncentral.org)
- National Reading Panel: Teaching Children to Read, National Institute of Child Health & Human Development (www.nichd.nih.gov/publications/nrp/smallbook.htm)
- Headsprout (www.headsprout.com)

In addition, several application-oriented journals describe teaching methods that have been supported through research. These include *Teaching Exceptional Children, The Reading*

Teacher, Intervention in School and Clinic, and *Journal of Applied School Psychology,* to name a few. Techniques described in these journals usually include a brief discussion about the research supporting the use of the technique and a detailed description of the implementation procedures and how they can be applied in the classroom.

WHAT CAN SCHOOL PSYCHOLOGISTS AND OTHER EDUCATIONAL CONSULTANTS DO?

1. Work with early childhood educators to include daily explicit instruction on the development of basic prereading and reading skills.
2. Help educators of older novice readers to infuse instructional time with skills that focus on the development of prereading and reading skills.
3. Help educators incorporate the teaching of basic reading skills by providing multiple practices in many contexts.
4. Encourage cross-age and peer tutoring and other types of assisted reading programs that increase students' opportunities to acquire basic reading skills.
5. Provide educators with an ongoing discussion about what constitutes evidence-based instruction and direct them to peer-reviewed resources that publish evidence-based instruction practices, such as peer-reviewed journals.
6. Facilitate educators' systematic inclusion of reading fluency exercises that use timed trials of repeated readings.
7. Collaborate with educators to develop data-recording charts and goal-attainment scales so that they are aware of when students have mastered skills or met reading achievement goals.
8. Help educators replace ineffective instructional practices with evidence-based ones.

SUMMARY POINTS

- Reading interventions that have a chance of meeting the needs of individual students are those that are scientifically based.
- Several different sound-manipulation activities may be used to teach phonemic awareness, such as sound isolation, sound substitution, sound deletion, sound addition, sound blending, and sound segmentation.
- Sound boxes can provide a scaffold for teaching segmentation skills.
- Nearly 500 words can be derived from thirty-seven rimes.
- Sorting words according to similar sound and letter sequence patterns may help children improve their spelling performance.
- Interspersing known and unknown words in students' reading may increase the number of words students attempt to read.
- *Phase drill* is an error-correction procedure that is used to promote students' generalization, or correct reading of words in connected text.
- Repeated readings increase fluency.

QUESTIONS FOR DISCUSSION

1. Discuss the concept of evidence-based interventions. How has federal legislation influenced the use of evidence-based interventions? How will educators access these interventions? How will the use of evidence-based reading practices meet students' needs?
2. Which word-reading techniques described in this chapter would you consider to be evidence-based and why?
3. Briefly explain how phonological awareness and phonic analysis techniques differ from whole word techniques.
4. How might a school psychologist or educator determine what type of intervention (phonological awareness, phonic analysis, or whole word) may be most appropriate for a given student?
5. How might educators incorporate peer tutoring activities within the reading programs discussed in this chapter?

REFERENCES

Adams, G. I., & Englemann, S. (1996). *Research on Direct Instruction: 25 Years Beyond DISTAR.* Seattle, WA: Educational Achievement Systems.

Adams, M. J. (1990). *Beginning to Read: Thinking and Learning about Print.* Cambridge, MA: MIT Press.

Ball, E., & Blachman, B. (1991). Does phonemic awareness training in kindergarten make a difference in early word recognition and developmental spelling? *Reading Research Quarterly, 26,* 49–66.

Banks, S. R., Guyer, B. P., & Guyer, K. E. (1993). Spelling improvement by college students who are dyslexic. *Annals of Dyslexia, 43,* 125–148.

Bear, D. R., Invernizzi, M. A., Templeton, S., & Johnston, F. (1996). *Words Their Way: Word Study for Phonics, Vocabulary, and Spelling.* Englewood Cliffs, NJ: Prentice Hall.

Bentin, S., & Leshem, H. (1993). On the interaction of between phonological awareness and reading acquisition: It's a two-way street. *Annals of Dyslexia, 43,* 125–148.

Blachman, B. A., Ball, E. W., Black, R., & Tangel, D. M. (2000). *Road to the Code: A Phonological Awareness Program for Young Children.* Baltimore: Brookes.

Bradley, L., & Bryant, P. E. (1983). Categorizing sounds and beginning to read—A causal connection. *Nature, 301,* 419–421.

Brown-Chidsey, R., & Steege, M. W. (2005). *Response to Intervention: Principles and Strategies for Effective Practice*. New York: Guilford Press.

Bryne, B., & Fielding-Barnsley, R. (1991). Evaluation of a program to teach phonemic awareness to young children. *Journal of Educational Psychology, 83,* 451–455.

Burns, M. K. (2004). Empirical analysis of drill ratio research: Refining the instructional level for drill tasks. *Remedial and Special Education, 25,* 167–173.

Burns, M. K., Dean, V. J., & Foley, S. (2004). Preteaching unknown key words with incremental rehearsal to improve reading fluency and comprehension with children identified as reading disabled. *Journal of School Psychology, 42,* 303–314.

Bursuck, W., & Dickson, S. (1999). Implementing a model for preventing reading failure: A report from the field. *Learning Disabilities Research & Practice, 14,* 191–202.

Carver, R. P. (1997). Reading for one second, one minute, or one year from the perspective of rauding theory. *Scientific Studies of Reading, 1,* 3–43.

Cates, G. L., Skinner, C. H., Watson, T. S., Meadows, T. J., Weaver, A., & Jackson, B. (2003). Instructional effectiveness and instructional efficiency as considerations for data-based decision-making: An evaluation of interspersing procedures. *School Psychology Review, 32,* 601–616.

Clark, D., & Uhry, J. (1995). *Dyslexia Theory and Practice Remedial Instruction*. Baltimore: New York Press.

Clay, M. (1993). *Reading Recovery: A Guidebook for Teachers in Training*. Portsmouth, NH: Heinemann.

Cunningham, P. M. (1995). *Phonics They Use: Words for Reading and Writing* (2nd ed.). New York: Harper Collins.

Cunningham, P. M. (1999). What should we do about phonics? In L. B. Cambrell, L. M. Morrow, S. B. Neuman, & M. Pressley (Eds.), *Best Practices in Literacy Instruction* (pp. 66–89). New York: Guilford Press.

Daly, E. J., III, Chafouleas, S., & Skinner, C. H. (2005). *Interventions for Reading Problems: Designing and Evaluating Effective Strategies*. New York: Guilford Press.

Daly, E. J., III, Lentz, F. E., & Boyer, J. (1996). The instructional hierarchy: A conceptual model for understanding the effective components of reading interventions. *School Psychology Quarterly, 11,* 369–386.

Daly, E. J., III, & Martens, B. K. (1994). A comparison of three interventions for increasing oral reading performance: Application of the instructional hierarchy. *Journal of Applied Behavior Analysis, 27,* 459–469.

Dangel, H. L. (1989). The use of student directed spelling strategies. *Academic Therapy, 25,* 43–51.

Downhower, S. (1987). Effects of repeated reading in second-grade transitional readers' fluency comprehension. *Reading Research Quarterly, 22,* 389–406.

Edelen-Smith, P. J. (1997). How now brown cow: Phoneme awareness activities for collaborative classrooms. *Intervention for School and Clinic, 33,* 103–111.

Elkonin, D. B. (1973). USSR. In J. Downing (Ed.), *Comparative Reading* (pp. 551–579). New York: Macmillan.

Englemann, S., & Bruner, E. (1988). *Reading Mastery I: DISTAR Reading.* Chicago: Science Research Associates.

Foorman, B., Francis, D., Beeler, T., Winikates, D., & Fletcher, J. M. (1997). Early interventions for children with reading problems: Study designs and preliminary findings. *Learning Disabilities, 8,* 63–71.

Gaskins, I. W., Downer, M. A., Anderson, R. C., Cunningham, P. M., Gaskins, R. W., Schommer, M., & The Teachers of Benchmark School (1988). A metacognitive approach to phonics: Using what you know to decode what you don't know. *Remedial and Special Education, 9,* 36–41.

Gillingham, A., & Stillman, B. W. (1997). *The Gillingham Manual: Remedial Training for Children with Specific Disability in Reading, Spelling, and Penmanship* (8th ed.). Cambridge, MA: Educators Publishing Service.

Goswami, U. (1986). Children's use of analogy in learning to read: A developmental study. *Journal of Experimental Child Psychology, 42,* 73–83.

Hale, A. D., Skinner, C. H., Winn, B. D., Oliver, R., Allin, J. D., & Molloy, C. M. (2005). An investigation of listening, listening-while-reading accommodations on reading comprehension levels and rates in students with emotional disorders. *Psychology in the Schools, 42,* 39–51.

Henry, M. K. (1998). Structured, sequential, multisensory teaching: The Orton legacy. *Annals of Dyslexia, 48,* 3–26.

Herman, P. A. (1985). The effect of repeated readings on reading rate, speech, pauses, and word recognition accuracy. *Reading Research Quarterly, 20,* 553–565.

Hohn, W. E., & Ehri, L. C. (1983). Do alphabet letters help prereaders acquire phonemic segmentation skill? *Journal of Educational Psychology, 75,* 752–762.

Johns, J. L., & Berglund, R. L. (2002). *Fluency: Strategies and Assessments* (2nd ed.). Dubuque, IA: Kendall/Hunt.

Johnston, F. R. (1999). The timing and teaching of word families. *The Reading Teacher, 53,* 64–75.

Joseph, L. M. (1998/1999). Word boxes help children with learning disabilities identify and spell words. *The Reading Teacher, 52,* 348–356.

Joseph, L. M. (2000a). Developing first-graders' phonemic awareness, word identification, and spelling: A comparison of two contemporary phonic approaches. *Reading Research and Instruction, 39,* 160–169.

Joseph, L. M. (2000b). Using word boxes as a large group phonics approach in a first-grade classroom. *Reading Horizons, 41,* 117–127.

Joseph, L. M. (2002). Facilitating word recognition and spelling using word boxes and word sort phonic procedures. *School Psychology Review, 31,* 122–129.

Joseph, L. M., & McCachran, M. (2003). Comparison of a word study phonics technique between students with moderate to mild mental retardation and struggling readers without disabilities. *Education and Training in Developmental Disabilities, 38,* 192–199.

Joseph, L. M., & Nist, L. (2006). Comparing the effects of unknown-known ratios on word reading learning versus learning rates. *Journal of Behavioral Education, 15,* 69–79.

Joseph, L. M., & Orlins, A. (2005). Multiple uses of a word study technique. *Reading Improvement, 42,* 73–79.

Juel, C., & Midden-Cup, C. (2000). Learning to read words: Linguistic units and instructional strategies. *Reading Research Quarterly, 35,* 458–489.

Keehn, S. (2003). The effect of instruction and practice through readers theater on young readers' oral reading fluency. *Reading Research and Instruction, 42,* 40–61.

Kennedy, K., & Blackman, J. (1993). Effectiveness of the Lindamood auditory discrimination in-depth program with students with learning disabilities. *Learning Disabilities Research & Practice, 8,* 253–259.

Knapp, N. F., & Winsor, A. P. (1998). A reading apprenticeship for delayed primary readers. *Reading Research and Instruction, 38,* 13–29.

Kratochwill, T. R., & Stoiber, K. C. (2002). Evidence-based interventions in school psychology: Conceptual foundations of the *Procedural and Coding Manual* of Division 16 and the Society for the Study of School Psychology Task Force. *School Psychology Quarterly, 17,* 341–389.

Kuhn, M. R., & Stahl, S. A. (2003). Fluency: A review of developmental and remedial practices. *Journal of Educational Psychology, 95,* 3–21.

Lewis-Snyder, G., Stoiber, K. C., & Kratochwill, T. R. (2002). Evidence-based interventions in school psychology: An illustration of task force coding criteria using group-based research design. *School Psychology Quarterly, 17,* 423–465.

Lindamood, C. H., & Lindamood, P. C. (1998). *Lindamood Phoneme Sequencing Program (LIPS).* Austin, TX: PRO-ED.

Lovett, M. W., Lacerenza, L., & Borden, S. L. (2000). Putting struggling readers on the PHAST track: A program to integrate phonological and strategy-based remedial reading instruction and maximize outcomes. *Journal of Learning Disabilities, 33,* 458–476.

Lovett, M. W., Lacerenza, L., Borden, S. L., Frijters, J. C., Steinback, K. A., & De Palma, M. (2000). Components of effective remediation for developmental reading disability: Combining phonological and strategy-based instruction to improve outcomes. *Journal of Educational Psychology, 92,* 263–283.

MacQuarrie, L. L., Tucker, J. A., Burns, M. K., & Hartman, B. (2002). Comparison of retention rates using traditional, drill sandwich, and incremental rehearsal flash card methods. *School Psychology Review, 31,* 584–595.

Maslanka, P., & Joseph, L. M. (2002). A comparison of two phonological awareness techniques between samples of preschool children. *Reading Psychology: An International Quarterly, 23,* 271–288.

McCormick, S. (1994). A nonreader becomes a reader: A case study for literacy acquisition by a severely disabled reader. *Reading Research Quarterly, 29,* 156–177.

McCormick, S. (Ed.). (2003). *Instructing Students Who Have Literacy Problems.* Upper Saddle River. NJ: Merrill/Prentice Hall.

McGuinness, D., McGuinness, C., & Donohue, J. (1995). Phonological training and the alphabet principle: Evidence for reciprocal causality. *Reading Research Quarterly, 30,* 830–852.

Mercer, C. D., Campbell, K. U., Miller, M. D., Mercer, K. D., & Lane, H. B. (2000). Effects of reading fluency intervention for middle schoolers with specific learning disabilities. *Learning Disabilities Research & Practice, 15,* 179–189.

Meyer, L. A. (1984). Long-term academic effects of the direct instruction project: Follow-through. *Elementary School Journal, 84,* 380–394.

Moran, D. J. (2004). The need for evidence-based educational methods. In D. J. Moran & R. Mallott (Eds.), *Evidence-Based Educational Methods* (pp. 3–5). New York: Elsevier Academic Press.

Morris, D., Shaw, B., & Perney, J. (1990). Helping low readers in grades 2 and 3: An after school volunteer tutoring program. *Elementary School Journal, 91,* 133–150.

National Association of School Psychologists. (2000). *Professional Conduct Manual: Principles for Professional Ethics and Guidelines for the Provision of School Psychological Services.* Bethesda, MD: Author. Retrieved from www.nasponline.org/pdf/ProfessionalCond.pdf

National Reading Panel. (2000). *Teaching Children to Read: An Evidence-Based Assessment of the Scientific Research Literature on Reading and Its Implications for Reading Instruction.* Washington, D.C.: National Institute for Literacy.

Neef, N. A., Iwata, B. A., & Page, T. J (1977). The effects of known-item interspersal on acquisition and retention of spelling and sight reading words. *Journal of Applied Behavioral Analysis, 10,* 738.

Neef, N. A., Iwata, B. A., & Page, T. J. (1980). The effects of interspersal training versus high-density reinforcement on spelling acquisition and retention. *Journal of Applied Behavior Analysis, 13,* 153–158.

Nelson, J. S., Alber, S. R., & Grody, A. (2004). Effects of systematic error correction and repeated readings on reading accuracy and proficiency of second graders with disabilities. *Education and Treatment of Children, 27,* 186–198.

No Child Left Behind Act of 2001 (2002). Public Law 107-110. 107th Congress of the United States of America. Retrieved from www.ed.gov/legislation/ESEAO2/107-110.pdf

O'Shea, L. J., Sindelar, P. T., & O'Shea, D. J. (1985). The effects of repeated readings and attentional cues on reading fluency and comprehension of learning disabled readers. *Learning Disabilities Research, 2,* 103–109.

Rasinski, T. V. (1990). Effects of repeated reading and listening while reading on reading fluency. *Journal of Educational Research, 87,* 158–164.

Rasinski, T. V. (2000). Speed does matter in reading. *The Reading Teacher, 54,* 146–151.

Roberts, M. L., & Shapiro, E. S. (1996). Effects of instructional ratios on students' reading performance in a regular education program. *Journal of School Psychology, 34,* 73–91.

Roberts, M. L., Turco, T. L., & Shapiro, E. S. (1991). Differential effects of fixed instructional ratios on students' progress in reading. *Journal of Psychoeducational Assessment, 9*, 308–318.

Ross, S. M., & Smith, L. J. (1994). Effects of the Success for All model on kindergarten through second grade reading achievement, teachers' adjustment, and classroom school climate at an inner-city school. *Elementary School Journal, 95*, 121–138.

Ross, S. M., Smith, L. J., Slavin, R. E., & Madden, N. A. (1997). Improving the academic success of disadvantaged children: An examination of Success for All. *Psychology in the Schools, 34*, 171–180.

Samuels, S. J. (1979). The method of repeated readings. *The Reading Teacher, 32*, 403–408.

Santa, C. M., & Hoien, T. (1999). An assessment of Early Steps: A program for early intervention or reading problems. *Reading Research Quarterly, 34*, 54–79.

Schmidgall, M., & Joseph, L. M. (in press). Comparison of phonic analysis and whole word reading on first graders' cumulative words read and cumulative reading rate: An extension in examining instructional effectiveness and efficiency. *Psychology in the Schools.*

Shapiro, E. S. (2004). *Academic Skills Problems: Direct Assessment and Intervention* 3rd. New York: Guilford Press.

Shernoff, E. S., Kratochwill, T. R., & Stoiber, K. C. (2002). Evidence-based interventions in school psychology: An illustration of task force coding criteria using single-participant research design. *School Psychology Quarterly, 17*, 390–422.

Simmons, D. C., & Kame'enui, E. J. (1998). *What Reading Research Tells Us About Children with Diverse Reading Needs: Bases and Basics.* Mahwah, NJ: Erlbaum.

Skinner, C. H. (2002). An empirical analysis of interspersal research evidence, implications, and applications of discrete task completion hypothesis. *Journal of School Psychology, 40*, 347–368.

Skinner, C. H., Adamson, K. L., Woodward, J. R., Jackson, R. R., Atchison, L. A., & Mims, J. W. (1993). The effects of models' rates of reading on students' reading during listening previewing. *Journal of Learning Disabilities, 26*, 674–681.

Slavin, R. E., Madden, N. A., Karwett, N. L., Dolan, L. J., & Wasik, B. A. (1992). *Success for All: A Relentless Approach to Prevention and Early Intervention in Elementary Schools.* Arlington, VA: Educational Research Service.

Stahl, S. A. (1992). Saying the "p" word: Nine guidelines for exemplary phonics instruction. *The Reading Teacher, 45*, 618–625.

Stoiber, K. C., & Kratochwill, T. R. (2001). Evidence-based intervention programs: Rethinking, refining, and renaming the new standing section of *School Psychology Quarterly*. *School Psychology Quarterly, 26*, 1–8.

Stoner, J. (1991). The potential for at-risk students to learn to read in groups contrasted under traditional and multisensory reading instruction. *Reading and Writing: An Interdisciplinary Journal, 3*, 19–30.

Tan, A., & Nicholson, T. (1997). Flashcards revisited: Training poor readers to read words faster improves their comprehension. *Journal of Educational Psychology, 89*, 276–288.

Therrien, W. J. (2004). Fluency and comprehension gains as a result of repeated reading: A meta analysis. *Remedial and Special Education, 25*, 252–261.

Topping, K. (1987). Paired reading: A powerful technique for parent use. *The Reading Teacher, 40*, 604–614.

Topping, K. (1995). *Paired Reading, Spelling, and Writing*. New York: Cassell.

Torgesen, J. K. (2001). Intensive remedial instruction for children with severe reading disabilities: Immediate and long-term outcomes from two instructional approaches. *Journal of Learning Disabilities, 34*, 33–59.

Tucker, J. A. (1988). *Basic Flashcard Technique When Vocabulary is the Goal.* Unpublished teaching material. Andrews University, Berrein Springs, MI.

U.S. Department of Education (n.d.). Proven methods. Retrieved from www.ed.gov/admins/tchrqual/evidence/whitehurst.html?exp=0

Wagner, R. K., Torgesen, J. K., Laughon, P., Simmons, K., & Raschotte, C. A. (1993). Development of young readers' phonological processing abilities. *Journal of Educational Psychology, 85*, 83–103.

Wagstaff, J. M. (1997). Building practical knowledge of letter-sound correspondences: A beginner's word wall and beyond. *The Reading Teacher, 51*, 298–304.

Weinstein, G., & Cooke, N. L. (1992). The effects of two repeated reading interventions on generalization of fluency. *Learning Disability Quarterly, 15*, 21–28.

Wise, B. W., Ring, J., & Olson, R. K. (1999). Training phonological awareness with and without explicit attention to articulation. *Journal of Experimental Child Psychology, 72*, 271–304.

Yopp, H. K. (1988). The validity and reliability of phonemic awareness tests. *Reading Research Quarterly, 23*, 159–177.

Yopp, H. K., & Yopp, R. H. (2000). Supporting phonemic awareness development in the classroom. *The Reading Teacher, 54,* 130–143.

Zutell, J. (1998). Word sorting: A developmental spelling approach to word study for delayed readers. *Reading and Writing Quarterly: Overcoming Learning Difficulties, 14,* 219–238.

Chapter 6

Comprehension Interventions

The main purpose of reading is to understand written communication and derive meaning from it. Much of the way events and information are communicated is in the form of written text. Technological advances have made written text a major form of communication; e-mail messages have practically replaced telephone calls for many things. Since more and more professional and personal business (meetings and presentations, health, banking, etc.) is conducted on the Internet, being literate is necessary for basic functioning in todays' technologically advanced society.

Poor readers do not have a repertoire of strategies for comprehending text. This affects their performance in almost all aspects of life. The National Reading Panel (2000) indicated that comprehension instruction is complex and should include the development of a variety of strategies for understanding information in narrative and expository texts (e.g., a novel or a science textbook). Therefore, instruction on strategies that facilitate obtaining meaning from text needs to be taught explicitly to these individuals. School psychologists and other educational consultants are in a good position to work with educators to foster the comprehension skills needed by students across content areas and classroom settings. Comprehension involves knowing the meanings of words, forming conceptual relationships, understanding factual or literal content, and making inferences.

VOCABULARY DEVELOPMENT

Children's vocabulary development has been associated with reading achievement (Catts, Fey, Zhang, & Tomblin, 2002; Scarborough, 1998). According to Nagy and Scott (2000), elementary children learn an estimated two thousand words per year at least.

Children, in general, will learn these words both implicitly and explicitly. Vocabulary development can be viewed as a "continuum from no knowledge; to a general sense, such as knowing that mendacious has a negative connotation; to narrow, context-bound knowledge; to having knowledge but not being able to access it quickly; to rich decontextualized knowledge of a word meaning" (Beck & McKeown, 1991, p. 792). Beck, McKeown, and Kucan (2002) described a similar continuum of deriving word meanings, which includes the following phases: (a) unknown (meaning is unfamiliar), (b) acquainted (meaning is derived after some thought), and (c) established (meaning is derived quickly and effortlessly). Children may derive meanings of words implicitly in connected text through the context of sentences, passages, or pictures (Watts, 1995). This may result in surface understandings of words rather than complete and deeper meanings of words. Children typically learn the meanings of five to fifteen words, out of approximately one hundred words they encounter in text (Swanborn & de Glopper, 1999). Many of these words are learned through free reading activities. Fluent readers tend to engage in free reading activities more often than nonfluent readers, and students have to engage in a substantial amount of connected text reading to learn a large number of word meanings (Baumann & Kame'enui, 1991).

Children who struggle with reading and understanding text need to be taught word meanings explicitly. It is highly likely that hundreds more words can be learned through direct vocabulary instruction (Stahl & Fairbanks, 1986). Direct instruction of vocabulary may involve different techniques: intensive instruction of a few words in a given lesson, (e.g., preteaching vocabulary using incremental rehearsal procedure as described in chapter 5) repeated exposure to and practice of the same word in multiple contexts, incorporation of gamelike activities to encourage children to learn meanings of words, and instruction on morphemic units or meaningful parts of words (Beck and McKeown, 1991; Carnine, Silbert, Kame'enui, & Tarver, 2004; Hittleman, 1983).

Other guidelines for teaching vocabulary were offered by Blachowicz and Fisher (1996) and Blachowicz and Lee (1991). They include teaching vocabulary words from the texts that students will be reading in the classroom, activating students' background knowledge by teaching new vocabulary words using analogies or synonyms, and using visual aids in text. Dictionary skills are important for helping children define words, but vocabulary instruction should not be limited to using the dictionary, because many words have multiple meanings and are used in a variety of ways to express ideas and events. Moreover, the exclusive use of dictionary exercises for introducing and understanding word meanings has not been found to be sufficient for learning vocabulary and comprehending text (Bos, Anders, Filip, & Jaffe, 1989). However, children should be taught to use the dictionary as a resource, because there are times when they will need to look up words to define them or confirm their meanings, such as when they are engaging in independent reading activities (Poindexter, 1994). For instance, a teacher may first have students write sentences using vocabulary words and then have them look up the words in the dictionary to determine if they had used the words appropriately in context (Rupley, Logan, & Nichols, 1998/1999).

TECHNIQUES FOR TEACHING VOCABULARY

School psychologists and other educational consultants can work collaboratively with educators to offer various techniques for helping children attain reading vocabulary. Although the various techniques provided here have been used by educators and have been described in the literature, more empirical research is needed to test their effectiveness.

Vocabulary Development During Storybook Reading

Storybook reading is an effective way for children to learn vocabulary words (Justice, Meier, & Walpole, 2005; Penno, Wilkinson, & Moore, 2002; Senechal, 1997). Vocabulary development occurs if the word appears more than once in the story. For instance, Robbins and Ehri (1994) found that children learned new words if the words appeared at least twice in the story, compared with words that appeared only once. Penno et al. (2002) found that children learned the meanings of words after they engaged in three repeated readings of storybooks. Having adults explain unfamiliar words during storybook reading has also been found to be effective for helping children develop meanings of words. For instance, during repeated reading lessons, Brett, Rothlein, and Hurley (1996) found that teachers' explanation of unfamiliar words, which included providing a definition and using the word in a sentence, significantly influenced fourth graders' vocabulary learning compared with the teacher providing no explanations when children were exposed to unfamiliar words in text.

Word Webs or Semantic Webs

Word webs, or semantic webs, use illustration to help students define and learn a word (Rupley et al., 1998/1999). Word or semantic webs can be used to introduce new vocabulary words before students read narrative or expository text that contain those words (see Figure 6-1). They can also be used after students have read text as a way of clarifying concepts or new vocabulary words presented in the text.

To use the technique, the instructor places the new vocabulary word or concept in the center of a blank space. The teacher guides the students in identifying other words that describe or relate to the new vocabulary word, such as adjectives, verbs, nouns, and synonyms. A circle is drawn around the word, and lines extend outward to other circles in which the descriptor words are placed. The teacher can ask the following questions to guide students: "What is it?" "What is it like?" "What are some examples?" "How are these examples the same or different?" The descriptor words can complete the center word. The students are then asked to state or write a definition of the word using the descriptors. Once this procedure is modeled by the instructor, students can create their own webs independently with instructor feedback. Word webs have been successfully used to teach vocabulary words (Dufflemeyer & Banwart, 1993).

Figure 6-1. *Word web of elements associated with the word "House."*

WORD WEB

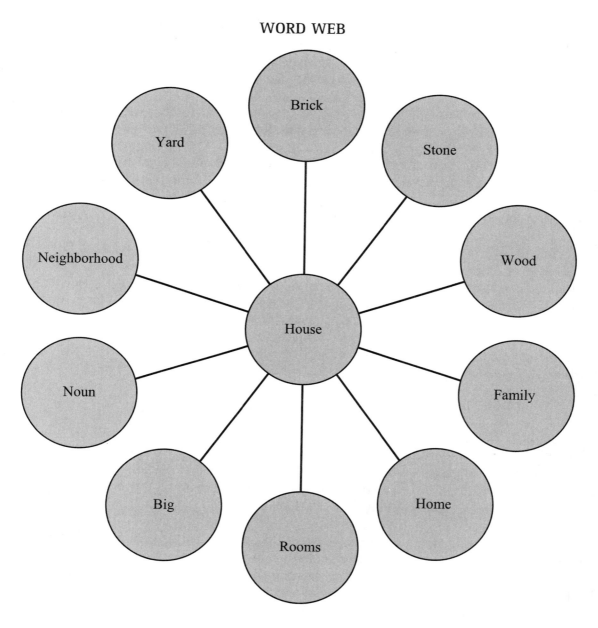

Process-Oriented Semantic Maps

Students who experience difficulty grasping conceptual relationship may find maps and diagrams to be helpful visual aids (Novak & Musonda, 1991). Process-oriented semantic maps are usually completed before students read narrative or expository text. The instructor guides the students in connecting concepts in a diagram format. Figure 6-2 is an example of

Figure 6-2. *Semantic map of the 1920s.*

SEMANTIC MAP

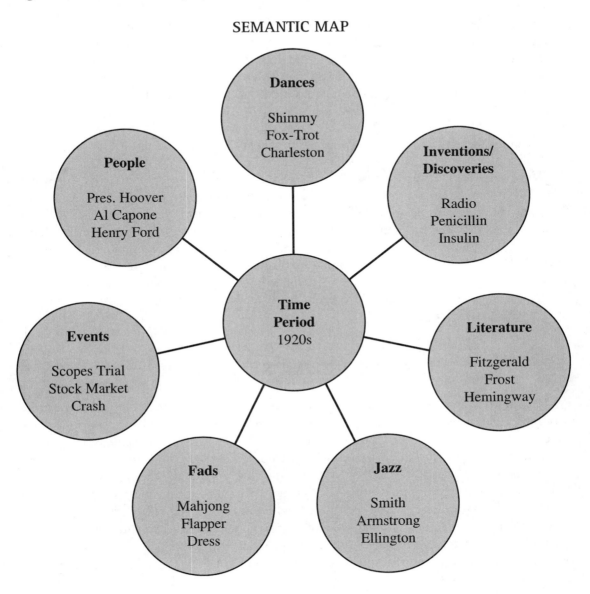

the topic and concepts related to the period of the 1920s. The teacher may ask the students questions such as "Who were the famous people of that period?" "What were the main events that took place?" "What were the main discoveries?" As the students respond to the questions, the teacher writes their responses on the diagram and draws a circle around them. This technique is designed to help students not only define the concept but also draw accurate inferences or meanings when this concept is expressed in text in the form of behaviors or characteristics.

Product-Oriented Semantic Maps

Product-oriented semantic maps are created after the students read the text. The teacher leads the students in diagramming concepts and making connections between them as a way of organizing the information they read. Product-oriented semantic maps can be used as graphic organizers to study and review before an exam about the readings. They also can be used as an assessment tool for determining if students have classified concepts appropriately and made accurate connections of content.

Meaning Sorts

Word sorts, which were described in chapter 5, are taught to help students sort words according to similar sound and spelling patterns. Words can also be sorted or categorized according to common meanings (Bear, Invernizzi, Templeton, & Johnston, 1996). For instance, words ending in "-ian," such as *physician*, *musician*, and *pediatrician*, can be classified under "people," and words ending in "-ion," such as *institution*, *nutrition*, and *education* can be classified under "things." Morphemic units such as affixes can also be classified according to common meaning categories; for instance, words beginning with the prefix "pre" are classified in the "before" category, and words beginning with "post" are categorized in the "after" category.

READING COMPREHENSION

Reading is "a process of communication by which a message is transmitted graphically between individuals." This early definition of reading comprehension was given by Kingston (1967, p. 72). Since then, transactional views of reading comprehension have surfaced that involve the interaction between what the reader brings to the text and the author's message (Pearson & Fielding, 1991). This view emphasizes the reader's active role in making meaning from text through a dialogue with the author's message. Pressley and Woloshyn, & Associates, (1995) articulated a general model for teaching students strategies for applying the transactional view of comprehending text. Their model emphasized teaching a few strategies at a time both intensively and extensively, demonstrating how to use each strategy, teaching the students where and when to use the strategies, having students practice using the strategies multiple times and in multiple contexts, having students monitor their use of strategies, and promoting generalization of strategy use by pointing out uses within various appropriate tasks during the school day. This general model of instruction has been used to teach students strategies of connecting text to prior knowledge and experiences, generating questions, constructing mental images, summarizing content, and predicting events (Pressley & El-Dinary, 1997).

The following section presents various reading comprehension strategies and techniques that have been found to be effective. School psychologists and other educational consultants can share and implement these with educators and parents.

Reading Comprehension Strategies and Techniques

The following examples of reading comprehension strategies and techniques are not exhaustive of the possible strategies and techniques, but they have been supported in the literature.

Question Generation

Research has shown that students improve their reading comprehension when they generate their own questions that they will answer in their reading (Mastropieri, Scruggs, Bakken, & Whedon, 1996). They can generate the questions before they read and use them to guide and monitor their understanding of text as they read. Story grammars can be used to generate questions and may include questions about the main characters, the characters' goals, the characters' obstacles in accomplishing their goals, and whether or not the characters reach their goals. Story grammars have been effective for improving reading comprehension performance (Johnson, Graham, & Harris, 1997). Other questions can be about the main ideas and other key elements in the text. Students are encouraged to read and reread text to answer their questions and to remember important contents from the text.

Summarizing Text

Students can use various summarization strategies to synthesize parts of text while they read. One summarization strategy is called *gist summaries*. Students are taught to restate important information using as few words as they can (fifteen words or less) to form one or two sentences about a paragraph of the text they just read. This activity is designed to help students retell the most important elements of the paragraph. The instructor gives feedback and guidance as the students refine their skills in creating gist summaries. This strategy has improved reading comprehension levels for general education students and students with disabilities (Simmons, Fuchs, Fuchs, Hodge, & Mathes, 1994).

Rinehart, Stahl, & Erickson (1986) used rule-governed summaries to summarize important information from sections of text. Their rules included deleting trivial and redundant information, composing a word to replace a string of words that describe an event, creating a topic sentence, and connecting important information. The teacher must define what constitutes important information, versus irrelevant and redundant information, before students begin this summarization activity. The teacher may also need to demonstrate creating topic sentences. After students complete their summary, they can check to see if they adhered to the rules and revise their summaries if they have not.

Hierarchical summaries involve surveying the entire reading selection while paying particular attention to the headings and subheadings in the text. Students construct an outline consisting of headings and subheadings, then list a main idea and two or three key words to describe the details in each subsection. Sentences are created using the key words. Students then write their summaries using the information from their outlines.

Taylor and Beach (1984) found this to be helpful for improving middle school students' reading comprehension of unfamiliar expository text.

Story Maps

Story maps can consist of grammars (characters, setting, and problem or plot in the story), which can be represented using graphic organizers (see figure 6-3). Having students do story mapping before, during, and after they read a story can help them attend to key elements of the story. The teacher makes a worksheet to create a graphic organizer on which students write down story elements (headings and subheadings), locating information in text as they read. The graphic organizer then serves as an organizational structure of key information from the story.

The teacher may need to demonstrate how to use the graphic organizer and provide guidance and feedback as students complete them on their own. Researchers have found story mapping to be an effective reading comprehension strategy for students with and without disabilities (Awe-Hwa, Vaughn, Wanzek, & Wei, 2004; Boulineau, Fore, Hagan-Burke, & Burke, 2004; Davis, 1994; Gardill & Jitendra, 1999; Idol, 1987; Vallecorsa & deBettencourt, 1997). Figure 6-3 provides an example of a very basic story map that may be used with younger children.

Passage Retell

Passage retell is often used to measure reading comprehension performance as described in chapter 3 of this book. However, passage retell can also be a reading comprehension strategy for understanding text and monitoring a student's understanding of text. Passage retell involves the student reading a passage and retelling that passage in his or her own words. Students can read a section or passage from a book and stop and retell that passage. They can then reread the passage to determine if they captured the essence of the passage. This is similar to paraphrasing what was read, which has been found to be effective in helping students improve their reading comprehension. Retellings can be oral or in writing.

Response Cards

The purpose of using response cards is to allow every student in the classroom to practice answering comprehension questions (Heward et al., 1996). Thus, it provides all students with opportunities to answer questions about the content presented in narrative or expository texts. The class is asked to read a story or sections from their textbooks. Afterward, they are presented with dry-erase boards, small chalkboards, or small poster boards. The teacher asks a question and the students write a response on their boards. The students hold up their boards for the teacher to view their responses. The teacher checks their responses and provides the correct answer verbally or on a board. Students check to see if their responses match their teacher's response. Preprinted cards with a number of

Figure 6-3. *Story mapping.*

Book Title	*Flap Your Wings*
Book Author	P. D. Eastman
Characters (Who?)	Mr. Bird, Mrs. Bird, Junior, and "A Boy"
Setting (Where?)	In a tree by the water.
Problem/Conflict (Focal point)	Mr. and Mrs. Bird find an egg in their nest that does not belong to them. When Junior is born, Mr. and Mrs. Bird have trouble satisfying his hunger. When Junior gets too big for the nest, he must learn to fly.
Events (What happened?)	A boy finds an egg on the ground and puts it in Mr. and Mrs. Bird's nest. Mr. and Mrs. Bird sit on the egg to keep it warm until the egg hatches. Mr. and Mrs. Bird collect a lot of food for Junior. Mr. and Mrs. Bird try to teach Junior to flap his wings and fly.
Resolution/Conclusion (Outcome)	Despite all efforts on the part of Mr. and Mrs. Bird, Junior cannot fly because he is not a bird, he is an alligator! Junior falls from the air and lands in the water beneath the tree where he can swim with the other alligators.
Theme (Main idea/Moral)	Love one another despite differences. Shown in the story through: Just because the egg did not belong to Mr. and Mrs. Bird didn't mean they should not take care of it. Mr. and Mrs. Bird learned that they could not expect Junior to fly, but they could celebrate how well he could swim!

possible responses can also be constructed and the students can clip a clothespin next to the correct or best response. This activity fosters active engagement in responding to comprehension questions. It has been used successfully to teach content area from texts (Heward et al., 1996).

KWL

KWL stands for "what you already *know*, what you *want* to learn, and what you have *learned*" (Ogle, 1986). Before reading narrative or expository text, students are asked to record responses on a sheet of paper with three columns, titled: What you already know; What you want to learn; and What you have learned. Before they read the text, they are given a general idea of what the text is about; then they record on a sheet of paper what they already know and what they want to learn about the subject. After they read the text, they record what they have learned from the text. The response they record in the column on what they have learned should be above and beyond what they already knew about the subject. They compare their responses in each column to determine if they learned more than they already knew and if they learned what they had hoped to learn. Jennings (1991) and McAllister (1994) found that the KWL technique was useful as a reading comprehension tool, both for learning and for assessment of learning.

PQ4R (Preview, Question, Read, Reflect, Recite, and Review)

The PQ4R method involves having students preview the reading material, question the reading, read to answer the questions, reflect on the reading, recite the reading, and review the content. Previewing the reading includes surveying the chapter titles, main topics, and subheadings of the text. The subheadings can be turned into questions that the student will answer by reading the text. Students reflect on the content as they read by pausing to form connections and create images (questions may serve as a prompt to reflect on content). Students recite by retelling what they remember about the readings. This helps them monitor how much information they are retaining from the reading. Students reread sections of the text that were not retained. Students then review the reading material, answer questions, and refer back to the text to clarify mistaken or incomplete responses. This method extends the former SQ3R (Survey, Question, Read, Recite, and Review) method by including the reflection phase (Thomas & Robinson, 1972).

Reciprocal Teaching

Reciprocal teaching is a reading comprehension approach that emphasizes teacher-student and student-student dialogues about reading material. The teacher asks a small group of students to read a chapter from the text. The teacher and students meet as a group to discuss the readings. The teacher initially leads the discussion by asking questions, clarifying responses, summarizing, and predicting. Once this process is modeled for the students, the group reads another section of the book and the students take turns leading the discussion by questioning, clarifying responses, summarizing what was read, and predicting the events that might occur in the book. Palinscar and Brown (1984) found this process to be helpful for delayed readers; in fact, they found that delayed readers even caught up with and exceeded their peers on reading comprehension performance.

Fostering of Reading Comprehension Through Self-Monitoring

For the purposes of this chapter, self-monitoring refers to students' use of data-recording procedures to assess or check their understanding of what they have just read (Mace & Kratochwill, 1988). In contrast with poor readers, good readers comprehend well because they self-monitor and consistently check for understanding. School psychologists and other educational consultants can facilitate the use of self-monitoring by making educators aware of various self-monitoring techniques.

Students can be taught to use direct and indirect data-gathering procedures to measure and foster reading comprehension (Joseph, 2005). Direct methods include frequency counts, latency measures, duration measures, and time-sampling measures. Frequency counts can involve recording the number of details the student provided in a retelling of a story. Students can then reread and retell passages and count how many more details they were able to retell to determine if they are improving. Students can also count the number of comprehension questions answered correctly and record this number, then reread the passage to see if they can increase the number of questions answered correctly. Additionally, they can count the number of times they look back in the text (text look-back) to determine how often they are having to check their understanding. *Latency measures* can be used to record how much time has elapsed before they begin to retell a passage or answer a comprehension question, and *duration measures* can be used to record how long it takes to retell a passage, answer comprehension questions, and construct a graphic organizer of contents from the passage. *Momentary sampling* can be used to divide into smaller intervals the amount of time allocated for completing comprehension activities. This type of recording procedure can be especially helpful for students who have difficulty staying on task while completing reading comprehension activities. For instance, a thirty-minute reading comprehension activity can be divided into six five-minute intervals. A timer can be set to beep every five minutes. Each time the beep is heard, students can record whether or not they are engaged (time on task) in the comprehension activity. This is a fixed-interval schedule. The timer can also be set for a variable-interval schedule.

Qualitative direct recording of reading comprehension behaviors can be used in conjunction with the quantitative data-recording procedures. Qualitative methods may be used to examine and reflect on the quality of the responses, that is, how well they depict the student's understanding of the text (Wade, Trathen & Schraw, 1990). Narration can involve students using oral (tape recorders) or written (journal) accounts of their understanding of the text. After they complete their narratives, they can evaluate them to determine if they have an in-depth understanding or a surface understanding of the text. They can also evaluate whether they express main ideas and facts about events or content, whether they interpret metaphors and make other types of inferences, and whether they predict events.

If they create graphic organizers, they can evaluate the content in that way. Scoring rubrics can also be used to evaluate answers to teachers' specific written comprehension questions.

Indirect data-recording methods involve self-rating (self-perceptions) of skills using, for instance, metacognitive awareness inventories. Inventories include a measure of reading behaviors that are rated using an ordinal scale. For example, quantitative values can be assigned to a scale, giving, for example, a score of 4 to reflect high-quality, detailed descriptions of events from a story, and a score of 1 to reflect low-quality descriptions of events from a story. A metacognitive awareness inventory, such as the Megacognitive Awareness of Reading Strategies Inventory (MARSI; Mokhtari & Reichard, 2002), consists of statements about thoughts, actions, and strategies that are associated with comprehending text material. Students respond to each item by circling a quantitative value that represents 1, "I never do this," to 5, "I always do this."

Direct and indirect methods can be used to not only evaluate quality and quantity of responses but also evaluate the effectiveness of a reading comprehension strategy that is used. The methods help determine whether the use of a particular strategy is responsible for developing high-quality interpretations of text or not. As students implement a reading comprehension strategy, they can use the various self-monitoring methods described in this section to determine if the strategies they have used are helping them improve their understanding of text.

Graphic representations of quantitative, qualitative, direct, and indirect data that are gathered should be used so students can evaluate their performance over time. Spreadsheets, charts, line graphs, bar graphs, or creative charting can be used, such as filling in a game board or moving along a race track. These types of graphic representations of data can help children view their progress and make decisions about the strategies they are using to gain meaning from text. In other words, data serve as a form of feedback on students' performance and whether their use of a certain strategy is helping them.

As part of the self-monitoring approach, students need to be taught to respond to this form of feedback. They should learn to first develop a plan to make necessary changes, which could be reading for in-depth understanding, using more text look-back, or selecting a different strategy that may be more effective and efficient for aiding their comprehension. Instructors can simultaneously chart performance and allow students to compare their own recordings of performance with their instructor's to determine if their observations and perceptions are similar or different. The instructor and student can discuss those differences, leading to improvement of the student's self-monitoring behaviors and more instructor guidance in strategy selection.

Self-monitoring may also occur when students realize they have made a mistake or when they want to confirm correct responses. Students can use various strategies, including self-checking, cross-checking one source against another, rereading to confirm a response, and rereading to solve a problem with their response (Schmitt, 2005). Engaging in self-monitoring behaviors and charting performance may help motivate or increase good reading behaviors (Paris & Winograd, 1990). Some students like to beat their last score; in other cases, self-monitoring methods may help students attribute their success to their own effort, rather than to some variable they cannot control. If they can attribute their success to their exhibiting desired reading behaviors, they may believe they are capable of further learning (that is, self-efficacy). Thus, it helps them engage in a process of continuous improvement and embark on the road to life-long learning. More research is needed to determine the differential effects of various self-monitoring methods across the different types of reading behaviors and skills (Joseph, 2005).

Self-monitoring behaviors can be applied across all types of literacy skills. They can also be used to evaluate the effectiveness of the strategies students are using to derive meaning from text. Many of the strategies and techniques described in this chapter and in chapter 5 incorporate self-monitoring of reading behavior.

WHAT CAN SCHOOL PSYCHOLOGISTS AND OTHER EDUCATIONAL CONSULTANTS DO?

1. Work with educators and parents to implement comprehension strategies and techniques that best address the individual needs of students.
2. Facilitate the direct teaching of strategies and the promotion of their use in multiple contexts.
3. Help educators develop systematic procedures for implementing and evaluating reading comprehension interventions.
4. Help educators and parents plan for additional practice and opportunities to comprehend text.
5. Work with educators who teach content area subjects other than reading and language arts and aid them in implementing comprehension strategies.
6. Share in the development of self-monitoring data-recording procedures that help students monitor their own reading behaviors and improve their skills.

SUMMARY POINTS

- Direct vocabulary instruction involves presenting a few words at a time, providing repeated practice of the same word in multiple contexts, and helping children understand morphemic units of words.
- Reading often and from a variety of print sources is an effective way to increase vocabulary.
- Word and semantic webs can help students form conceptual relationships.
- Reading comprehension is transactional because it involves the interaction between what the reader brings to the text and the author's message.
- Question generation, summarization of text, story maps, and passage retell are among the strategies students can use to comprehend text.

- Students who comprehend text will engage in self-monitoring behaviors.
- Self-monitoring reading behaviors can use quantitative or qualitative methods.

QUESTIONS FOR DISCUSSION

1. Why is vocabulary development a critical component of reading comprehension?
2. Discuss how reading comprehension strategies may be used as instructional tools as well as for assessing learning and performance.
3. Do any of the reading comprehension strategies and techniques discussed in this chapter draw on students' prior knowledge? Explain.
4. Describe direct and indirect data-gathering methods for measuring and fostering reading comprehension. Discuss the purposes for each of the methods and explain why both should be used.
5. Briefly explain how self-monitoring methods can be incorporated in reading interventions. Give an example of how this might be done.

REFERENCES

Awe-Hwa, K., Vaughn, S., Wanzek, J., & Wei, S. (2004). Graphic organizers and their effects on the reading comprehension of students with LD: A synthesis of research. *Journal of Learning Disabilities, 37*, 105–118.

Baumann, J. F., & Kame'enui, E. J. (1991). Research on vocabulary instruction: Ode to Voltaire. In J. Flood, D. Lapp, & J. R. Squire (Eds.), *Handbook of Research on Teaching English Language Arts* (pp. 604–632). New York: Macmillan.

Bear, D. R., Invernizzi, M. A., Templeton, S., & Johnston, F. (1996). *Words Their Way: Word Study for Phonics, Vocabulary, and Spelling.* Englewood Cliffs, NJ: Prentice Hall.

Beck, L., & McKeown, M. (1991). Conditions of vocabulary acquisition. In R. Barr, M. Kamil, P. Mosenthal, & P. D. Pearson (Eds.). *Handbook of Reading Research* (Vol. 2, pp. 789–814). New York: Longman.

Beck, I. L., McKeown, M. G., & Kucan, L. (2002). *Bringing Words to Life: Robust Vocabulary Instruction.* New York: Guilford Press.

Blachowicz, C., & Fisher, P. (1996). *Teaching Vocabulary in All Classrooms.* Upper Saddle River, NJ: Merrill/Prentice Hall.

Blachowicz, C., & Lee, J. (1991). Vocabulary development in the literacy classroom. *The Reading Teacher, 45*, 188–195.

Bos, C. S., Anders, P. L., Filip, D., & Jaffe, L. E. (1989). The effects of an interactive instructional strategy for enhancing reading comprehension and content area learning for students with learning disabilities. *Journal of Learning Disabilities, 22,* 384–390.

Boulineau, T., Fore, C., Hagan-Burke, S., & Burke, M. D. (2004). Use of story-mapping to increase the story-grammar text comprehension of elementary students with learning disabilities. *Learning Disabilities Quarterly, 27,* 105–120.

Brett, A., Rothlein, L., & Hurley, M. (1996). Vocabulary acquisition from listening to stories and explanations of target words. *Elementary School Journal, 96,* 415–422.

Carnine, D. W., Silbert, J., Kame'enui E. J., & Tarver, S. G. (Eds.). (2004). *Direct Instruction Reading* (4th ed.) Upper Saddle River, NJ: Pearson.

Catts, H. W., Fey, M. E., Zhang, X., & Tomblin, J. B. (2002). A longitudinal investigation of reading outcomes in children with language impairments. *Journal of Speech, Language, and Hearing Research, 45,* 1142–1157.

Davis, Z. T. (1994). Effects of prereading story-mapping on elementary readers' comprehension. *Journal of Educational Research, 87,* 353–360.

Dufflemeyer, F. A., & Banwart, B. H. (1993). Word maps for adjectives and verbs. *The Reading Teacher, 46,* 351–353.

Gardill, M. C., & Jitendra, A. K. (1999). Advanced story-map instruction. Effects on the reading comprehension of students with learning disabilities. *Journal of Special Education, 33,* 2–17.

Heward, W. L., Gardner, R., III, Cavanaugh, S. S., Courson, F. H., Grossi, T. A., & Barbetta, P. M. (1996). Everyone participates in this class: Using response cards to increase active student response. *Teaching Exceptional Children, 28,* 4–10.

Hittleman, D. R. (1983). *Developmental Reading, K-8: Teaching from a Psycholinguistic Perspective* (2nd ed.). Boston: Houghton Mifflin.

Idol, L. (1987). Group story mapping: A comprehension strategy for both skilled and unskilled readers. *Journal of Learning Disabilities, 20,* 196–205.

Jennings, J. H. (1991). A comparison of summary and journal writing as components of an interactive comprehension model. In J. Zutell & S. McCormick (Eds.), *Learner Factors/ Teacher Factors: Issues in Literacy Research and Instruction* (pp. 67–82). Chicago: National Reading Conference.

Johnson, L., Graham, S., & Harris, K. R. (1997). The effects of goal setting, self-instruction on learning a reading comprehension strategy: A study of students with learning disabilities. *Journal of Learning Disabilities, 30,* 80–91.

Joseph, L. M. (2005). The role of self-monitoring in literacy learning. In S. E. Israel, C. C. Block, K. L. Bauserman, & K. Kinnucan-Welsch (Eds.), *Metacognition in Literacy Learning* (pp. 199–214). Mahwah, NJ: Erlbaum.

Justice, L. M., Meier, J., & Walpole, S. (2005). Learning new words from storybooks: An efficacy study with at-risk kindergarteners. *Language, Speech, and Hearing Services in Schools, 36,* 17–32.

Kingston, A. (1967). Some thoughts on reading comprehension. In L. Hafner (Ed.), *Improving Reading Comprehension in Secondary Schools* (pp. 72–75). New York: MacMillian.

Mace, F. C., & Kratochwill, T. R. (1988). Self-monitoring: Applications and issues. In J. Witt, S. Elliot, & F. Gresham (Eds.), *Handbook of Behavior Therapy in Education,* (pp. 489–502). New York: Pergamon.

Mastropieri, M. A., Scruggs, T. E., Bakken, J. P., & Whedon, C. (1996). Reading comprehension: A synthesis of research in learning disabilities. In T. E. Scruggs & M. A. Mastropieri (Eds.). *Advances in Learning and Behavioral Disabilities* (Vol. 10, pp. 277–303). Greenwich, CT: JAL.

McAllister, P. (1994). Using K-W-L for informal assessment. *The Reading Teacher, 47,* 510–511.

Mokhtari, K., & Reichard, C. A. (2002). Assessing students' metacognitive awareness of reading strategies. *Journal of Educational Psychology, 94,* 249–259.

Nagy, W. E., & Scott, J. A. (2000). Vocabulary processes. In M. L. Kamil, P. B. Mosenthal, P. D. Pearson, & R. Barr (Eds.), *Handbook of Reading Research* (Vol. 3, pp. 269–284). Mahwah, NJ: Erlbaum.

National Reading Panel. (2000). Teaching children to read: An evidence-based assessment of the scientific research literature on reading and its implications for reading instruction. Retrieved on July 26, 2005 from www.nichd.nihgov/publications/nrp./smallbook.htm

Novak, J. D., & Musonda, D. (1991). A twelve-year longitudinal study of science concept learning. *American Educational Research Journal, 28,* 117–154.

Ogle, D. M. (1986). K-W-L: A teaching model that develops active reading of expository text. *The Reading Teacher, 39,* 564–570.

Palinscar, A. S., & Brown, A. L. (1984). Reciprocal teaching of comprehension-fostering and comprehension monitoring activities. *Cognition and Instruction, 1,* 117–175.

Paris, S. G., & Winograd, P. (1990). How metacognition can promote academic learning and instruction. In B. F. Jones & L. Idol (Eds.). *Handbook of Reading Research* (Vol. 3, pp. 545–561). Hillsdale, NJ: Erlbaum.

Pearson, D., & Fielding, L. (1991). Comprehension instruction. In B. Barr, M. Kamil, P. Mosenthal, & P. D. Pearson (Eds.), *Handbook of Reading Research* (Vol. 2, pp. 815–860). New York: Longman.

Penno, J. F., Wilkinson, I. A., & Moore, D. W. (2002). Vocabulary acquisition from teacher explanation and repeated listening to stories. Do they overcome the Matthew effect? *Journal of Educational Psychology, 94,* 23–33.

Poindexter, C. (1994). Guessed meanings. *Journal of Reading, 37,* 420–422.

Pressley, M., & El-Dinary, P. B. (1997). What we know about translating comprehension strategies into practice. *Journal of Learning Disabilities, 30,* 486–488.

Pressley, M., & Woloshyn, V., & Associates. (1995). *Cognitive Strategy Instruction That Really Works with Children* (2nd ed.). Cambridge, MA: Brookline.

Rinehart, S. D., Stahl, S. A., & Erickson, L. G. (1986). Some effects of summarization training on reading and studying. *Reading Research Quarterly, 21,* 422–438.

Robbins, C., & Ehri, L. C. (1994). Reading storybooks to kindergarteners helps them learn new vocabulary words. *Journal of Educational Psychology, 86,* 54–64.

Rupley, W. H., Logan, J. W., & Nichols, W. D. (1998/1999). Vocabulary instruction in a balanced reading program. *The Reading Teacher, 52,* 336–346.

Scarborough, H. S. (1998). Early identification of children at risk for reading difficulties: Phonological awareness and some other promising predictors. In B. K. Shapiro, P. J. Accardo, & A. J. Capute (Eds.), *Specific Reading Disability: A View of the Spectrum* (pp. 75–199). Timonium, MD: York Press.

Schmitt, M. C. (2005). Measuring students' awareness and control of strategic processes. In S. E. Israel, C. C. Block, K. L. Bauserman, & K. Kinnucan-Welsch (Eds.), *Metacognition in Literacy Learning* (pp. 101–119). Mahwah, NJ: Erlbaum.

Senechal, M. (1997). The differential effect of storybook reading on preschooler's acquisition of expressive and receptive vocabulary. *Journal of Child Language, 24,* 123–138.

Simmons, D. C., Fuchs, D., Fuchs, L. S., Hodge, J. P., & Mathes, P. G. (1994). Importance of instructional complexity and role reciprocity to classwide peer tutoring. *Learning Disabilities Research & Practice, 9*, 203–212.

Stahl, S. A., & Fairbanks, M. M. (1986). The effects of vocabulary instruction: A model-based meta-analysis. *Review of Educational Research, 56*, 72–110.

Swanborn, M. S. L., & de Glopper, K. (1999). Incidental word while reading: A meta-analysis. *Review of Educational Research, 69*, 261–285.

Taylor, B. M., & Beach, R. W. (1984). The effects of text structure instruction on middle-grade students' comprehension and production of expository text. *Reading Research Quarterly, 19*, 134–146.

Thomas, E. L., & Robinson, H. A. (1972). *Improving Reading in Every Class: A Sourcebook for Teachers.* Boston: Allyn & Bacon.

Vallecorsa, A. L., & deBettencourt, L. U. (1997). Using a mapping procedure to teach reading and writing skills to middle grade students with learning disabilities. *Education and Treatment of Children, 20*, 173–189.

Wade, W., Trathen, W., & Schraw, G. (1990). An analysis of spontaneous study strategies. *Reading Research Quarterly, 25*, 147–166.

Watts, S. (1995). Vocabulary instruction during reading lessons in six classrooms. *Journal of Reading Behavior, 27*, 399–424.

Chapter 7

Conducting Functional Analyses
of Reading Performance

School psychologists, educational consultants, and educators have an ethical obligation to rise above the fads, politics, and personal biases that dominate policy making with regard to educational practices. The National Association of School Psychologists' *Professional Conduct Manual* (2000) asserts that school psychologists need to take responsibility for making data-based decisions, implementing evidence-based interventions, and ensuring that the efficacy of interventions is evaluated. The current NASP standards for training school psychologists also emphasize that university programs should teach and evaluate prospective school psychologists' understanding and use of data-based decision-making processes.

Odgen R. Lindsley, a prominent scholar, was instrumental in helping educators who work in applied settings to move away from basing decisions on personal perceptions and instead base decisions on objective data from student performance (Kennedy, 2005). The objective data-gathering techniques he developed are used to assess students' reading performance and to determine if instruction methods are producing desired changes in students' reading performance. (The terms *reading behavior* and *reading performance* are used interchangeably in this chapter.)

Data-based decision making, plus demonstration of accountability and responsibility for educational practices, involves techniques that use a functional approach to understanding reading behavior. In a functional approach involving experimental or cause-and-effect methods, practitioners analyze what comes before (antecedents) and after (consequences) students' reading performance (Daly, Witt, Martens, & Dool, 1997). Antecedents and consequences are external events, or factors, that are under the control of the educator and can be altered or manipulated to bring about desired changes in students' reading performance (Daly, Witt, et al., 1997). As components of reading instruction or interventions, antecedents and consequences can be implemented or altered before and after a student performs a reading skill. Thus, they need to be tested by conducting functional or experimental analyses to determine their effect on student reading performance (Daly, Witt, et al., 1997).

School psychologists and other educational consultants can use assessment methods described in chapter 3 to help teachers determine the effectiveness of interventions and instructional components described in chapters 4, 5, and 6.

Evidence-based reading interventions and effective teaching components (such as those described in chapters 4, 5, and 6, which match students' reading skill needs) may increase the likelihood that the interventions will be effective for meeting those needs. However, the actual effectiveness of those interventions needs to be tested. Functional or experimental analyses involve scientifically sound procedures for testing the effectiveness of interventions on an individual's and on a group of students' reading performance (Daly, Persampieri, McCurdy, & Gortmaker, 2005). In other words, functional or experimental analyses of reading performance determine if interventions, instruction, particular components of instruction, or strategies designed to improve reading behavior, do in fact produce desirable reading performance outcomes. Daly, Persampieri, et al. (2005) indicated that practitioners would be able to adhere to national, state, and local educational data-based accountability standards if they used experimental or functional analyses procedures.

FUNCTIONAL OR EXPERIMENTAL ANALYSES TO TEST INTERVENTIONS AND COMPONENTS OF INSTRUCTION

Several interventions have been designed to help students improve their reading skills, some of which were described in chapters 5 and 6. Also, chapter 4 described several components of effective instruction or interventions, for example, modeling, opportunities to respond, corrective feedback, and reinforcement. Because of the limited amount of time allocated for instruction in schools, teachers need to be efficient in delivering instruction. Therefore, not all of the interventions and components of effective instruction will be needed or applicable for helping individual students achieve desired outcomes. For instance, one student may know how to perform a reading task but is not yet fluent, so that student does not need to have the skill modeled but needs more opportunities to practice it. Some children may have an application (won't do) rather than a skill (can't do) problem. According to Daly, Persampieri, et al. (2005), children may need incentives or rewards for completing reading tasks, or they may need more practice when they are not performing a reading skill at a proficient level. On the other hand, skill or acquisition problems may require modeling or error correction. When a child is referred for reading problems, it is not obvious to the teacher which components the child requires in order to improve reading performance. Effective instructional components that are considered likely to produce the desired reading performance need to be tested for individual students to determine whether they will be appropriate.

Brief functional or experimental analysis has been used to test the effectiveness of interventions when time constraints are involved, such as in schools or other applied settings (e.g., Harding, Wacker, Cooper, Millard, and Jensen-Kovalan, 1994). Since 1994, others have extended the use of brief functional analysis to address academic performance problems (Daly, Martens, Dool, & Hintze, 1998; Daly, Martens, Hamler, Dool, & Eckert, 1999; Hendrickson, Gable, Novak, & Peck, 1996).

Witt, Daly, and Noell (2000) described a model for conducting a brief functional analysis and testing effective instructional components. Their model involves the following steps: (1) determining the desired performance outcome and how it will be measured, (2) selecting the instructional components and ordering them from easiest to hardest, (3) determining how instructional components will be implemented and tested across conditions, (4) using an evaluation design to determine the effectiveness of the instructional components, and (5) measuring and interpreting the results reliably.

Determining the Desired Performance Outcome

When a student is referred for reading skill problems, school psychologists in collaboration with educators need to determine the desired reading performance outcome, such as the student will accurately read one hundred words per minute on grade-level passages. This outcome needs to be stated in specific, observable, and measurable terms and address the clear evaluation of the conditions in which instructional components are implemented. There should be a direct link between the child's expected performance and the skills to be taught using instructional components (Daly, Witt, et al., 1997). For instance, if a student is expected to read a passage quickly and accurately, then the instructional component can be modeling of reading the passage accurately and quickly, providing repeated practice reading the passage, or providing corrective feedback on words read inaccurately during passage reading.

Selecting the Instructional Components

School psychologists and educational consultants can use functional analysis to help teachers select and create a list of instructional components that may produce desired reading outcomes. According to Witt et al. (2000), these components can be classified as antecedents or consequences. For instance, modeling is typically used as an antecedent when teaching a new skill. The teacher may demonstrate how to decode a word before the children are asked to decode the word. In this instance, corrective feedback can be used as a consequence if the teacher corrects the students' inaccurate attempts to decode a word.

Once the teachers, in collaboration with educational consultants, have created a list of potential instructional components, they may order the components from easiest to hardest to implement, with regard to the amount of assistance needed and how well the component fits into the existing instructional routine (Witt et al., 2000). Research has supported the use of rank ordering from easiest to hardest to implement for use with academic instructional components (Daly, Martens, Dool, et al., 1998; Daly, Martens, Hamler, et al., 1999).

More importantly, rank ordering of instructional components may be completed according to a student's stage of learning. Students may be at an acquisition, fluency, generalization, or adaptation stage of learning to read. This form of rank ordering is better known as the instructional hierarchy (Daly, Chafouleas, & Skinner, 2005). Students at an acquisition stage of learning need instruction that focuses on increasing skills that are new to them. If they are having difficulty decoding a word, they may need to be directly taught phonic analysis skills. Once students are able to use these skills—increasing their skills in reading words accurately and decreasing inaccurate reading of words—they need instruction designed to build fluency so that they not only read words accurately but also read them quickly and effortlessly. This fluency instruction may entail repeated timed trials on reading words accurately. Once fluency has been achieved, instruction is next targeted at helping students generalize the reading of words in multiple contexts (various types of narrative and expository texts). Finally, students' reading skills may be extended to decoding new words that may contain the same phonic patterns as the words they have mastered. This is referred to as adapting the skill to learning new content.

In many cases, teachers may find it difficult to identify which stage the student is functioning at within the instructional hierarchy. To match appropriate reading instruction with the students' reading skill needs, educators may need to conduct a functional or experimental analysis to identify appropriate instructional components that facilitate students' reading skill acquisition, fluency, generalization, and adaptation.

Determining How Instructional Components Will Be Implemented and Tested

A process called *stacking* can be used to test the effectiveness of instructional components (Witt et al., 2000). This process involves defining a baseline condition in which no instructional component is provided. The second condition contains the easiest instructional component to be implemented; the third condition contains the easiest and the next easiest in the hierarchy, and so forth up to the final condition that contains all components from easiest to hardest. For example, if instructional components consisted of (from easiest to hardest) listening passage preview (modeling), repeated reading (practice), and phase drill (corrective feedback), then the following conditions may be stacked: (1) listening passage preview, (2) listening passage preview and repeated readings, and (3) listening passage preview, repeated readings, and phase drill. In empirical investigations, instructional components have been tested using stacking procedures (Daly, Martens, Hamler, et al., 1999; Daly, Murdoch, Lillenstein, Webber, & Lentz, 2002) and compared within an instructional hierarchy framework (e.g., Daly & Martens, 1994; Daly, Lentz, & Boyer, 1996).

The validity of an intervention or components of instruction is threatened when the integrity of the implementation is compromised (Sanetti & Kratochwill, 2005). In some cases, interventions have been found to be ineffective because they did not adhere to all the implementation procedures (Telzrow & Beebe, 2002). Therefore, educational consultants need to make sure that the instructional components are implemented as planned. For instance, educators responsible for implementing listening passage preview should adhere to all procedures for this component. Also, observed procedures of instruction need to be recorded to document that the instruction was implemented with integrity or as designed. An observation form can be used that includes a list of the materials, operationally defined procedures, instructional context or setting, and instructional time. The observer records whether these elements of the intervention were adhered to (yes or no) and the degree of adherence (Sanetti & Kratochwill, 2005). School psychologists and other educational consultants can play the role of independent observer and provide praise and constructive corrective feedback on the instructors' implementation of procedures.

Using an Evaluation Design to Determine the Effectiveness of the Instructional Components

Scientists have used single-subject experimental designs successfully to answer empirical questions. In the medical profession, for instance, researchers and practicing physicians use these designs to help them determine the effects of a treatment and if, what, when, and how changes in treatment need to be made.

Single-subject designs can be used to test the effectiveness of reading instruction with individual students as well as with a group of students. According to McCormick (1995), analysis of data is personalized for each individual, whether he or she is receiving the intervention alone or with other students in a small or large group. She further states, "The goal is to demarcate each individual's current level or stage of responses at the beginning of an experiment and then to determine the degree in which approaches examined in the investigation change each individual's responses" (p. 4). Single-subject designs have been used to test the effectiveness of reading interventions for many years (see Neuman & McCormick, 1995).

In applied settings such as schools, it is difficult to determine the effectiveness of an instructional method using control-comparison group experimental designs. Yet it is important for educators to answer the question: Are the instructional methods that are implemented making a difference in student performance? Steege, Brown-Chidsey, and Mace (2002) described several advantages for school psychologists and other educational consultants who use single-subject designs. These include conducting multiple measurements of outcome variables before and during intervention, documenting students' progress objectively; evaluating interventions over time, making it possible to identify effective and ineffective components of instruction so that changes can be made; and complying with federal, state, and professional ethical guidelines for documenting student performance in response to instruction. For comparisons to be made, conditions need to be similar but independent of each other in terms of the specific content being taught so that the results in one condition do not influence results in another condition (i.e., treatment interference; Daly, Witt, et al., 1997). In other words, the same words or the same reading passage may not be presented across conditions, but words taught and passages used should be of equal difficulty level across conditions so that accurate comparisons can be made and to ensure that performance outcome differences between conditions are not due to the difficulty level of the content taught in the various conditions (Daly, Witt, et al., 1997). The results of these repeated measures are typically depicted on line graphs to permit a visual analysis of the data; in particular, trends in the data path become apparent. Several types of single-subject designs can be used to test effectiveness of reading instruction: basic case study designs, reversal designs, multiple baseline designs, alternating treatment designs, and repeated acquisition designs. These designs should be taught to prospective educational practitioners as well as to those currently practicing.

Basic Case Study Designs

Basic case study designs are referred to as baseline ("A") and intervention ("B") designs. In this design, the reading performance outcome measure is conducted repeatedly until a stable trend in reading performance is demonstrated. Reading intervention, instruction, or another instructional component is then introduced (the intervention phase, and the reading performance outcome measure is again conducted repeatedly to determine if a change in performance trend is observed during the intervention phase. Figure 7-1 illustrates a basic case study (AB) design involving the number of words read accurately on flashcards during a "no specialized instruction" condition (baseline) and during a "corrective feedback instruction" condition (intervention). AB designs cannot be used to demonstrate a functional relation between the intervention and the students' reading performance. It is mainly used when circumstances prevent the use of other designs. However, it can be used to track changes in performance over time, although it is difficult to determine if the intervention was responsible for the change (Steege et al., 2002). If the goal is to test the effectiveness of reading interventions or instruction, the other single-subject designs should be used, because experimental control can be demonstrated.

Reversal Designs

Reversal designs are sometimes called withdrawal designs (Steege et al., 2002). They begin with the same procedures as AB designs, but the intervention is withdrawn for a short period of time, and there is a return to baseline conditions followed by a return to intervention conditions (ABAB designs). Figure 7-2 illustrates a reversal design when story mapping is used to help answer comprehension questions from reading a passage. In this example, a fifth-grade student was asked to orally read passages and answer comprehension questions during the initial baseline condition. During the intervention condition, he was asked to

Figure 7-1. *Basic case study (AB) design.*

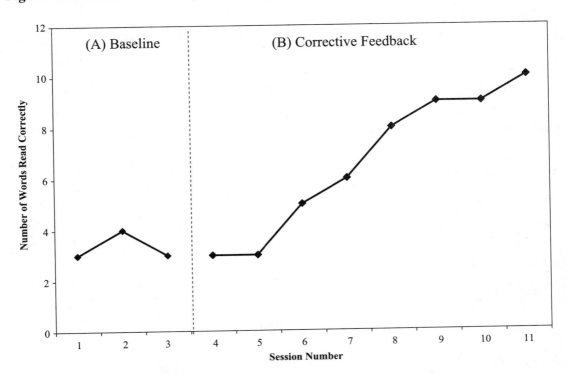

orally read passages, create a story map, and then answer comprehension questions. To determine if the story map affected the student's answering of the comprehension questions, the instructor removed the use of a story map and a return to baseline conditions, in which the fifth grader read the passage orally and answered comprehension questions. The use of the story map was reintroduced in the return-to-intervention condition so the student could return to experiencing success in answering comprehension questions. Passages read across conditions were different to minimize intervention interference but were similar in difficulty level to minimize confounding influences of outcome measures.

The use of this design is problematic in demonstrating a functional relation when the skills that are being taught cannot be unlearned. This is often the case when measuring reading skill performance. In other words, once intervention or instruction is withdrawn, many reading skills cannot be unlearned. Therefore, reversal designs are very powerful in demonstrating a functional relation between the intervention or instruction and student behavior, but these designs may not be the best to use when academic performance is the behavior of interest.

An example of using a reversal or withdrawal design is a study conducted by Lalli and Shapiro (1990). These investigators studied the effects of self-monitoring and contingent reward-on-sight word acquisition for eight students with learning disabilities. A return to baseline occurred on three occasions in between the conditions of feedback, self-monitoring, and self-monitoring plus contingent reward.

Figure 7-2. Reversal (ABAB) design.

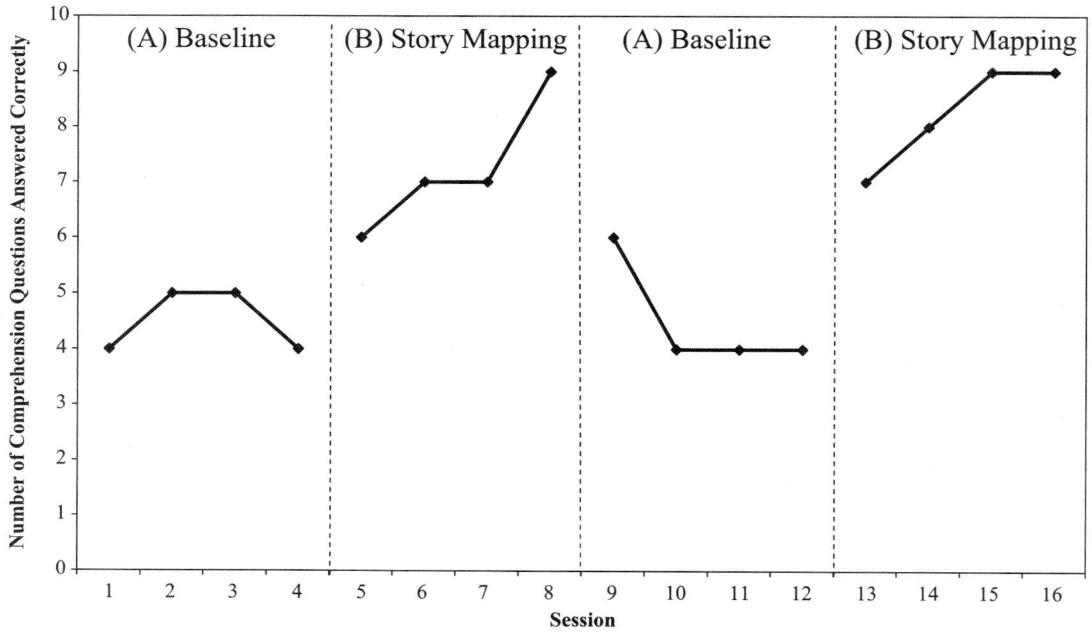

Multiple Baseline Designs

In multiple baseline design, two or more baselines are identified, and the intervention is introduced sequentially and staggered across baselines. There are usually three tiers of baselines and three tiers of intervention phases (Kennedy, 2005). This design can be implemented across reading skills and across settings in which reading skills are required. For instance, a procedure involving word-sorting phonic analysis (discussed in chapter 6) could be implemented across baseline measurements of the following three word reading skills: (a) single-syllable word sets, (b) two-syllable word sets, and (c) three or more syllable word sets. Another instance may involve the use of a story map across baseline measurements of comprehension in students' reading, social studies, and science classes. When a desired change in performance occurs only when the intervention is present, a functional relation is established (Kennedy, 2005). An example of a literacy study using multiple baseline designs is one conducted by Shapiro and McCurdy (1989). These researchers used a multiple baseline design across subjects to determine if a taped word-modeling format could foster improvement in high school students with behavior problems.

Alternating Treatment Designs

Sometimes referred to as multielement designs, alternating treatment designs are used to examine the effects of two or more interventions to determine if they produce

Figure 7-3. *Alternating treatment design.*

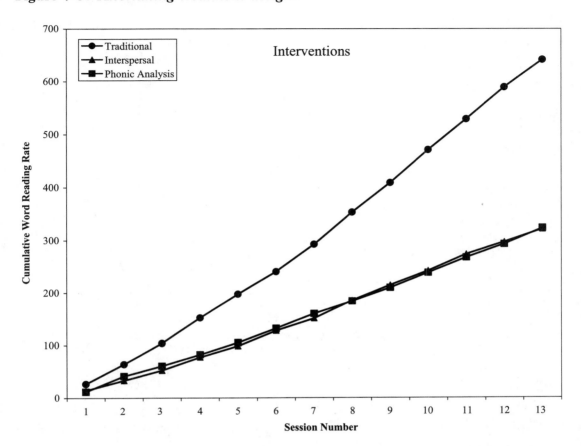

differentiated results. Interventions are presented in a counterbalanced, rapidly alternating order. Differentiation in performance needs to occur between intervention conditions or among intervention conditions to demonstrate a functional relation. Figure 7-3 provides an example of a multielement design in which a traditional drill and practice, an interspersal procedure, and a phonic analysis procedure were presented in alternating fashion to compare results on measures of word learning rates. As can be seen from the illustration, word learning rate performance was distinctively different under traditional drill and practice than performance under the other two intervention conditions.

When using this design to compare the effectiveness of reading interventions, one must be aware of the potential effects of multiple-intervention interference that can occur across conditions for any particular student. Rose and Beattie (1986) used an alternating treatment or multielement design to study the effects of two instructional conditions on the number of words read correctly by four students. In one of the instructional conditions, the teacher read a passage orally while the students followed along. In another condition, students listened to a tape-recorded reading of the passage as they followed along.

Figure 7-4. *Repeated acquisition design.*

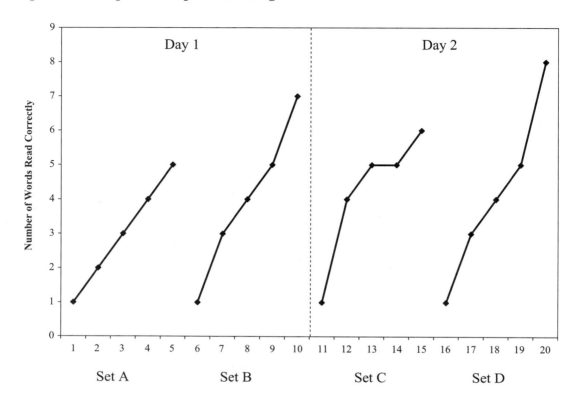

A continuing baseline condition consisting of no specialized instruction was simultaneously implemented throughout the study.

Repeated Acquisition Designs

When the analysis of skill acquisition under different intervention conditions is the objective, the use of repeated acquisition designs may be the most beneficial for examining differential effects of two or more intervention conditions. These designs involve using multiple equivalent learning tasks and examining acquisition repeatedly from one task to another under at least two different intervention conditions (Kennedy, 2005). Barbetta, Heward, Bradley, and Miller (1994) used a repeated acquisition design to study differential effects of delayed and immediate practice on acquisition of sight words. Each week, seven words were randomly assigned to the immediate and delayed practice interventions. The process was repeated until one of the sets of words was acquired. Findings revealed that three out of four students reach acquisition levels on sight words in the immediate practice conditions first. This finding was demonstrated both within student performance and across students on several sets of sight words. Figure 7-4 is a hypothetical example using a repeated acquisition design to show improvement in reading performance.

Measuring and Interpreting the Results Reliably

An evaluation of the data when conducting an experimental analysis requires examining whether differences in reading performance have occurred between baseline and intervention conditions. First and foremost, progress monitoring data should be recorded on paper or on a data-based management spreadsheet. Plotting reading performance under baseline and intervention conditions on a line graph can provide a visual inspection of the data points to determine if a difference in reading performance occurred between the two conditions. The use of line graphs makes it possible to communicate reading performance results in a clear, objective, and precise manner to interested stakeholders such as parents.

Presenting results in this way also communicates the value of assessing the effectiveness of interventions because it allows interested stakeholders to view changes, if there are any, from condition to condition. If there is overlap between data points in baseline and intervention conditions, chances are that reading performance did not differ, which means that the intervention did not produce a positive change in reading performance. Brown-Chidsey and Steege (2005) point out that it is difficult to determine if improvements have occurred during intervention conditions if 20 percent or more of the data points overlap with those obtained in the baseline condition.

According to Witt et al. (2000), change in reading performance level, trend, and variability may be analyzed. A change in level means that the patterns of data points of baseline and intervention are similar, except the pattern in intervention conditions is clearly at a higher level ("raised up") than in baseline. For example, a student may read an average of two words, with a range of zero to three words correct, during baseline and read an average of eight words correct with a range of seven to ten words correct during intervention conditions. In some instances, changes in performance trend may be evident during the intervention phase, usually when a steadily increasing trend of data points occurs above those observed in baseline phases. For instance, a student doing repeated readings may increase his or her oral reading fluency at a slower rate than when that student is doing repeated readings combined with phase drill instruction. Changes in performance variability may occur between baseline and intervention conditions when, for instance, the data points do not fluctuate from high to low levels in baseline as dramatically as they do during intervention phases. For example, a student may fluctuate on the number of correct responses to comprehension questions from session to session to a larger degree during sessions when paraphrasing strategy was used than during baseline conditions.

Functional or experimental analyses using the various single-subject designs can be used to test the effectiveness of reading interventions with individual students, small groups of students, and large class sizes (Barnett, Daly, Jones, & Lentz, 2004). The use of these types of analysis and evaluation procedures has been promoted in particular when incorporating a response-to-intervention model that uses scientifically based systematic procedures for targeting and monitoring reading instruction (interventions) and assessing performance outcomes of individuals, small groups, and large classrooms of pupils (see Brown-Chidsey & Steege, 2005).

Using Functional (Experimental) Analysis in a Response-to-Intervention (RTI) Model

In 2004, the reauthorization of the Individuals with Disabilities Education Improvement Act (IDEIA) and No Child Left Behind Act (NCLB) of 2001 emphasized that the quality of instructional environments and the students' response to those environments would be assessed and evaluated. Many leading scholars in the field of school psychology and related disciplines have proposed using a response-to-intervention model for assessing the instructional environment using student academic performance measures (Brown-Chidsey & Steege, 2005; Fuchs & Fuchs, 1998). These scholars operationalized a framework that was originally articulated in the 1982 National Research Council report (Heller, Holtzman, & Messick, 1982). A response-to-intervention model (RTI) is a data-based decision-making process in which interventions (classwide and individual) are determined on the basis of student performance data. Valid interventions are identified after they have been implemented and their effects sequentially monitored (Daly, Persampieri, et al., 2005). Three tiers of instruction and three phases of assessment have been described in response-to-intervention models (Brown-Chidsey & Steege, 2005; Fuchs & Fuchs, 1998). The three tiers represent a continuum of the intervention intensity needed to produce appropriate responsiveness, as measured by students' academic performance. A study conducted by Daly, Persampieri, et al. (2005) illustrates a way to test students' responsiveness to reading interventions using an experimental analysis of academic performance that uses a research-to-practice perspective. The three tiers are discussed here in relation to reading performance.

The first tier of instruction involves classwide, scientifically based reading instruction that is designed to foster reading competence (Brown-Chidsey & Steege, 2005). If this is done at the school district level, it may involve curriculum coordinators, administrators, reading specialists, and general and special educators all searching for reading methods and programs that have been scientifically supported and selecting those that would best meet the population of students in their district. Once scientifically based reading methods or programs are selected, they need to be implemented and assessed systematically and consistently across classrooms (Brown-Chidsey & Steege, 2005).

Assessment of this first tier of instruction involves the administration of a reliable and valid curriculum-based measure (e.g., DIBELS or AIMSWEB) of reading performance to establish baseline levels at the beginning of the school year and to monitor reading progress during the school year (Fuchs, 2003). DIBELS was described in chapter 3 of this book. Educators can use curriculum-based measures to measure reading performance progress during the school year and determine if changes in instruction need to occur. Brown-Chidsey and Steege (2005) recommend that benchmark data be gathered at least at the beginning, middle, and end of the school year. If the class is performing below other classes in the building, then a different type of reading instruction or more effective instructional components need to be incorporated or incorporated more frequently. Brown-Chidsey and Steege (2005) suggest that those students who are performing at the bottom 16 to 25 percent of the class may need to be provided with intervention. Reading performance progress continues to be monitored. Students that did not respond at an expected level with tier 1 types of instruction need supplementary instruction and are provided with tier 2 reading instruction.

Tier 2 reading instruction involves supplementary scientifically based reading interventions that are targeted to meet specific reading skill needs. For example, instruction may include small group instruction that gives students more practice reading words accurately in connected text by providing additional phase drill exercises (see a description of this technique in chapter 5). These additional word reading practice activities can be facilitated by the classroom teacher, an instructional aid, an intervention specialist, an older student, or a competent peer. Tier 2 also includes more frequent assessment and monitoring of progress in reading performance.

According to Brown-Chidsey and Steege (2005), single-subject case designs can be used to monitor students' responsiveness to tier 2 supplementary reading instruction. Stated another way, experimental or functional analysis can be conducted to determine if the supplementary reading instruction is resulting in a positive change in reading performance. Essentially, progress monitoring is conducted to determine if students are reaching benchmark standards. The use of experimental or functional analysis will allow educators to make data-based decisions when they are considering making changes in instruction. Changes in instruction may be in relation to the intensity, duration, or frequency of an intervention or may involve replacing the intervention with another (Brown-Chidsey & Steege, 2005). Several tier 2 reading interventions should be tried before determining that the student is not benefiting from this tier of service delivery. However, if substantial instruction does not produce desired reading performance outcomes in this tier, practitioners should provide students with more intensive scientifically based reading instruction. That intervention usually involves one-on-one instruction, extended instructional time, and a significant increase in the number of opportunities to receive instruction and practice on specific reading skills.

Children who need tier 3 instructional services, unlike their peers, did not benefit from universal and supplemental types of instruction implemented in general education classrooms. These students will typically receive more comprehensive assessment to determine if they are eligible for special education services in reading (Brown-Chidsey & Steege, 2005; Fuchs & Fuchs, 1998). If students are identified as having a learning disability in the area of reading, or as having other types of disabilities that involve acquisition of or fluency in reading, and they are placed in a special education program or another type of pull-out program, functional analysis of reading interventions still needs to be conducted. In other words, it is critical to implement systematic data-gathering procedures to determine whether a type of reading instruction is meeting the needs of individual students in all types of classroom settings. All educators and support service personnel need to be accountable for students' reading achievement.

RTI models have been effective for helping students improve their reading performance (Martson, Muyskens, Lau, & Canter, 2003; O'Connor, Harty, & Fulmer, 2005; Speece, Case, & Malloy, 2003). Other research has suggested that the three-tiered process described in the RTI model has been effective for identifying children who may need special education services (Fletcher et al., 2002; Fuchs, 2003) and appears to be a promising approach in preventing academic difficulties, especially if implemented in the primary grades (Brown-Chidsey & Steege, 2005). However, more empirical investigations need to be conducted to test the validity of this model for assessing and evaluating the effects of different types of reading instruction.

Likewise, practitioners need to be provided with some suggestions for dealing with the challenges they may face when implementing this model. For instance, the multiple skills involved in reading need to be taught, tracked, and recorded, making data-gathering activities potentially cumbersome. Teaching skills to students systematically so that one skill builds on another decreases the complex and potentially cumbersome data-collection process. Although instruction of reading skills is often a linear or sequential process, it also needs to occur in a fluid and meaningful ("rich") way. In other words, there are instances in which reading skills, such as forming conceptual relationships, are embedded in other contexts, such as content area reading exercises. Consultants and educators need to have a solid understanding of the multitude of reading skills and how they are related so that the various aspects of reading are assessed and targeted for intervention. Collateral effects of an intervention also need to be assessed, as well as reading behaviors in addition to areas that may be influenced by the intervention.

The types of reading assessments available for tracking the performance of multiple reading skills are limited. Over the past decade, assessment of skills such as reading fluency, word identification, and phonemic awareness has improved. However, there is a lack of valid measurement tools for assessing other reading skills. Although some questions need to be answered regarding the use of an RTI model such as the one proposed by Brown-Chidsey and Steege (2005), the model's principles and practices of directly linking assessment to intervention have been found to be effective by many prominent scholars in the field of school psychology and related disciplines. Therefore, school psychologists and educational consultants may wish to seriously consider using functional analysis procedures to test the effectiveness of interventions on the reading progress of students who experience challenges acquiring reading skills and becoming proficient readers.

WHAT CAN SCHOOL PSYCHOLOGISTS AND OTHER EDUCATIONAL CONSULTANTS DO?

1. Help school districts realize the value of evaluating the effectiveness of reading interventions as a major assessment component.

2. Facilitate the selection and implementation of evidence-supported reading interventions and instructional components.
3. Share in the development and implementation of methods to evaluate instructional effectiveness.
4. Ensure that interventions are implemented with integrity.
5. Facilitate the use and understanding of graphic and other data representations of performance.
6. Facilitate the making of instructional decisions based on reading performance data.
7. Work at the systems, building, and classroom levels to implement response-to-intervention models for all students.

SUMMARY POINTS

- Decisions about instruction should be based on data rather than on perceptions (they should be evidence-based).
- Functional or experimental analyses involve determining the desired performance outcome, selecting and ordering instructional components from easiest to hardest, implementing and testing instructional components, using an evaluation design to determine the effectiveness of instructional components, and reliably measuring and interpreting the results.
- Instructional components that are selected, implemented, and tested can include, for instance, modeling and demonstration, corrective feedback, repeated practice, and positive reinforcement.
- *Stacking* instructional components refers to beginning with the easiest component, progressing to a slightly more difficult component, and eventually implementing all components from easiest to hardest if desired outcomes are not met along the way.
- Single-subject designs such as reversal, multiple baseline, alternating treatment, and repeated acquisition can be used to establish a functional relationship between intervention and change in reading performance.
- The level, trend, and variability of performance are recorded and analyzed.
- Instructional analysis can be used in a tiered response-to–intervention (RTI) process for targeting children in need of intensive reading intervention.

QUESTIONS FOR DISCUSSION

1. Give an example of an antecedent and a consequence of reading behavior.
2. Discuss ways in which consultants can help educators implement interventions with consistency and integrity.
3. What are some advantages and some drawbacks of using single-subject designs in reading research?
4. Briefly define RTI and discuss how functional analysis can be incorporated into each tier.
5. Provide an example of stacking instructional components and describe the circumstances in which this method might be useful.

REFERENCES

Barbetta, P. M., Heward, W. L., Bradley, D. M., & Miller, D. (1994). Effects of immediate and delayed error correction on the acquisition and maintenance of sight words by students with developmental disabilities. *Journal of Applied Behavior Analysis, 27,* 177–178.

Barnett, D. W., Daly, E. J., Jones, K., & Lentz, F. E. (2004). Response to intervention: Empirically based special service decisions from single-case designs of increasing and decreasing intensity. *Journal of Special Education, 38,* 66–79.

Brown-Chidsey, R., & Steege, M. W. (2005). *Response to Intervention: Principles and Strategies for Effective Practice.* New York: Guilford Press.

Daly, E. J., III, Chafouleas, S., & Skinner, C. H. (2005). *Interventions for Reading Problems: Designing and Evaluating Effective Strategies.* New York: Guilford Press.

Daly, E. J., III, Lentz, F. E., & Boyer, J. (1996). The instructional hierarchy: A conceptual model for understanding the effective components of reading interventions. *School Psychology Quarterly, 11,* 369–386.

Daly, E. J., III, & Martens, B. K. (1994). A comparison of three interventions for increasing oral reading performance: Application of the instructional hierarchy. *Journal of Applied Behavior Analysis, 27,* 459–469.

Daly, E. J., III, Martens, B. K., Dool, E. J., & Hintze, J. M. (1998). Using brief functional analysis to select interventions for oral reading. *Journal of Behavioral Education, 8,* 203–218.

Daly, E. J., III, Martens, B. K., Hamler, K. R., Dool, E. J., & Eckert, T. L. (1999). A brief experimental analysis for identifying instructional components needed to improve oral reading fluency. *Journal of Applied Behavior Analysis, 32,* 83–94.

Daly, E. J., III, Murdoch, A., Lillenstein, L., Webber, L., & Lentz, E. (2002). An examination of methods for testing treatments: Conducting brief experimental analyses of the effects of instructional components on oral reading fluency. *Education and Treatment of Children, 25,* 288–316.

Daly, E. J, III, Persampieri, M., McCurdy, M., & Gortmaker, V. (2005). Generating reading interventions through experimental analysis of academic skills: Demonstration and empirical evaluation. *School Psychology Review, 34,* 395–414.

Daly, E. J., III, Witt, J. C., Martens, B. K., & Dool, E. J. (1997). A model for conducting a functional analysis of academic performance problems. *School Psychology Review, 26,* 554–574.

Fletcher, J. M., Foorman, B. R., Boudousquie, A., Barnes, M. A., Schatshneider, C., & Francis, D. J. (2002). Assessment of reading and learning disabilities: A research-based intervention oriented approach. *Journal of School Psychology, 40,* 27–63.

Fuchs, L. S. (2003). Assessing intervention responsiveness: Conceptual and technical issues. *Learning Disabilities Research & Practice, 18,* 172–186.

Fuchs, L. S., & Fuchs, D. (1998). Treatment validity: A unifying concept for reconceptualizing the identification of learning disabilities. *Learning Disabilities Research & Practice, 13,* 204–219.

Harding, J., Wacker, D. P., Cooper, L. J., Millard, T., & Jensen-Kovalan, P. (1994). Brief hierarchical assessment of potential treatment components with children in an outpatient clinic. *Journal of Applied Behavior Analysis, 27,* 291–300.

Heller, K. A., Holtzman, W. H., & Messick, S. (Eds.). (1982). *Placing Children in Special Education: A Strategy for Equity.* Washington, D.C.: National Academy Press.

Hendrickson, J. M., Gable, R. A., Novak, C., & Peck, S. (1996). Functional assessment as strategy assessment for teaching academics. *Education and Treatment of Children, 19,* 257–271.

Kennedy, C. H. (2005). *Single-Case Designs for Educational Research.* Boston, MA: Pearson.

Lalli, E. P., & Shapiro, E. S. (1990). The effects of self-monitoring and contingent reward on sight word acquisition. *Education and Treatment of Children, 13,* 129–141.

Martson, D., Muyskens, P., Lau, M., & Canter, A. (2003). Problem-solving model for decision-making with high incidence disabilities: The Minneapolis experience. *Learning Disabilities Research & Practice, 18,* 187–200.

McCormick, S. (1995). What is single subject experimental research? In S. B. Neuman & S. McCormick (Eds.), *Single Subject Experimental Research: Applications for Literacy* (pp. 1–31). Newark, DE: International Reading Association.

National Association of School Psychologists. (2000). Professional conduct manual: Principles for professional ethics and guidelines for the provision of school psychological services. Bethesda MD: Author. Retrieved from www.nasponline.org/pdf/Professional/Cond.pdf

Neuman, S. B., & McCormick, S. (1995). *Single Subject Experimental Research: Applications for Literacy.* Newark, DE: International Reading Association.

O'Connor, R. E., Harty, K. R., & Fulmer, D. (2005). Tiers of intervention in kindergarten through third grade. *Journal of Learning Disabilities, 38,* 532–538.

Rose, T. L., & Beattie, J. R. (1986). Relative effects of teacher-directed and taped previewing on oral reading. *Learning Disability Quarterly*, 9, 193–199.

Sanetti, L. H., & Kratochwill, T. R. (2005). Treatment integrity assessment within a problem-solving model. In R. Brown-Chidsey (Ed.), *Assessment for Intervention: A Problem-Solving Approach* (pp. 304–328). New York: Guilford Press.

Shapiro, E. S., & McCurdy, B. L. (1989). Effects of a taped-words treatment on reading proficiency. *Exceptional Children*, 55, 321–325.

Speece, D. L., Case, L. P., & Malloy, D. E. (2003). Responsiveness to general education instruction as the first gate to learning disabilities identification. *Learning Disabilities Research & Practice*, 18, 147–156.

Steege, M., Brown-Chidsey, R., & Mace, F. C. (2002). Best practices in evaluating interventions. In A. Thomas & J. Grimes (Eds.), *Best Practices in School Psychology IV* (pp. 517–534). Bethesda, MD: National Association of School Psychologists.

Telzrow, C., & Beebe, J. (2002). Best practices in facilitating intervention adherence and integrity. In A. Thomas & J. Grimes (Eds.), *Best Practices in School Psychology IV* (pp. 503–516). Bethesda, MD: National Association of School Psychologists.

Witt, J. C., Daly, E. M., III, & Noell, G. (2000). *Functional assessments: A Step-by-Step Guide to Solving Academic and Behavior Problems*. Longmont, CO: Sopris West.

Index